Stella's Quilt

Stella's Quilt

by Sherry Kenney

Paperback ISBN: 979-8-9868615-0-0
Library of Congress Control Number: 2023900416

Hester Press
Denver, Colorado
Inquiries: HesterPressCo@gmail.com

Book design: YellowStudios
Cover quilt pattern credit: Leanne Harvey (@leanne_mountvincentquilts)

First Edition
Printed in the United States of America

For Stella, with all the love
a grandmother's heart can hold.

Contents

Introduction

Grandmother Hester's quilts were not particularly beautiful. They were patchwork, made from squares of discarded clothes and fabric samples. But they were resilient, intended for warmth and protection from the bitter north wind that swept down through the Texas panhandle and crept in through the cracks. They were given to members of her own family, as well as to the families she and my grandfather sponsored for citizenship through their church, and to others in need. They were donated to shelters and orphanages. I loved climbing into bed at my grandparents' house under a pile of quilts—loved the sense of security they made me feel.

The pandemic year of 2020 was the worst of some people's lives, but it was the best of mine, because I got myself a little granddaughter, Stella Irene Berv. She was an outgoing baby with an amazing cowlick—every day was crazy hair day for Stella. Though my daughter, Lauren, and her husband, Alex, are both introverts, Stella's first word at seven months was "hi", which she gleefully exclaimed to everyone she encountered. Stella is going to try to make friends with the whole world. I want Stella to know who she is and whose she is. That is my goal for this book. This is not a history or a genealogy, but a collection of memories, stories, and impressions, collected from both sides of her family.

The metaphor of "quilt" began to tickle my brain during a Zoom happy hour with family members in the autumn of that worst/best COVID-19 year. Here were my beloved people, each one of them in a little square on the screen of my laptop—my children and my infant granddaughter, my three brothers and their wives, their children and grandchildren, my sister, my two Hester cousins, one cousin's husband, their son, and his girlfriend. That day one nephew was in Montreal; one niece joined in from Vilnius, Lithuania and the other from Mexico City. We were isolated…but connected.

There is a chart used by many financial institutions called "the quilt of diversification", or sometimes simply, "The Quilt". It illustrates the concept that asset classes move in and out of favor and that to achieve success an investor must own assets across a broad financial spectrum. In other words, a portfolio is strengthened by diversity. I view families the same way, and celebrate the strength and diversity among the Hesters, the Kenneys, the Beards, and the Bervs. We are Jewish, Catholic, Protestant, charismatic, agnostic, and atheist. We are gay and straight. We are Black, Asian, Latino, and Caucasian. We are bi-polar, dyslexic, brilliant, and on the spectrum. We are creative, artistic, and athletic. We love each other and cover each other with warmth and acceptance. We are Stella's quilt.

Part One

The Blocks

Sherry Gail Hester Kenney

Nana

I WAS BORN THE last day of the decade, December 31, 1949, in Lubbock, Texas—the hub of the South Plains, the home of the Texas Tech Red Raiders, and the buckle of the Bible Belt. My earliest memory is of my parents, Ross Wyatt and Elizabeth Ruth (Betty) Hobbs Hester, taking me to an urgent care clinic on a Sunday afternoon for stitches. I had been sitting in my stroller when one of my father's younger cousins, who lived next door, accidentally ran over the top of my right foot on his bicycle. I still have the scar.

We lived in the house my father had built in 1952, when I was two, with help from my mother's younger brother, Eldon Hobbs. The front of the house ran perpendicular to busy Forty-sixth Street and featured a concrete front porch that extended for the length of the house. This porch was often the venue for my parents' parties, on which occasion they sprinkled it with dance wax for easier gliding. Mother and Daddy were both excellent dancers; she later taught ballroom dance lessons for Arthur Murray Dance Studio.

Mother organized the neighborhood children for talent shows and plays that we performed on the front porch "stage". She loved theater, and was a talented director, actor, singer, costume designer and stagehand. She volunteered with the Lubbock Little Theater, an amateur community theater, where she acted in *South Pacific*, the 1949 Rodgers and Hammerstein Broadway hit. She sang *I'm Gonna Wash That Man Right Outa My Hair* until we all had it memorized. Mother took opera lessons from a voice instructor who came to our house, and she sang solos in our church choir. Her taste in music ran from majestic hymns, to *Faust* and *Carmen,* to "Hit Parade" tunes.

Our front porch was also the site of my Uncle David Hester's marriage to Billie Hotchkiss Laman. By that time, I had three younger siblings—Randal Ross, Debra Renée, and Stephen Keith—each of us approximately two years apart. Steve was seven weeks old when we learned, on November 15, 1956, there would be a wedding at our house that day. In a letter to her sister-in-law, Sybil Horne, my grandmother wrote that David had stopped by his parents' home in the evening to tell them he was getting married the next morning. She and Granddaddy picked up a bakery cake on their way to our house. She goes on to write that when Steve woke up, Mother did not have time to nurse him (nursing a baby was not done publicly in those days), so Grandmother gave him a bottle of sugar water. The best part of this surprise event was that Billie had a son, Melvin, who was just six months older than Randy, and we had our first cousin. Randy and Mel were the best of friends until our cousin died in 2016. Years later we learned that Billie, an accountant, had run a Dun & Bradstreet report on David before agreeing to marry him.

Billie and David broke ground for a house two lots east of ours, next to Keith and Ruth Ann Cass, good friends of my parents, who lived on the corner. Keith was a manager at my grandfather's store; my brother Steve is named for him. The Cass family had three children, Pamela, Bob, and Kemp. The house to the west of us, which Daddy's cousins, Minnie Mae Galloway and her three children, had moved from, was bought by Bill and Joyce Tarver, who had three children, Pamela, Gary, and Mike. The two Pams and I were the same age, and regular playmates.

Recently, my cousin Karen was going through family things after her father, Uncle David, died, and she sent a few items to me. Among them was a story my mother had written about an incident that occurred during this time. According to her narrative, a dirty and tearful five-year-old Randy came into her bedroom while she was getting ready for church one spring Sunday morning. He angrily asked why she had not come to help him, even though, he said, "I called and called for you." She tried to soothe him, but after consecutive nights of Randy sitting up in bed, screaming "Somebody please come help me!", she went in search of the reason. At my uncle's lot, a lone shovel stood against one wall of the cellar that had been dug for his new house. Mother took Randy back with her, where he explained that he had fallen in, called repeatedly for help, and when no one came, positioned the shovel against the dirt wall, climbed to the very top of it, and in sheer desperation clawed his way out of the hole.

During this traumatic event, my brother had not been missed, but not out of parental neglect. These were the days when children roamed freely about their neighborhood. If one of your children was not at home, you assumed he or she was at the home of one of your friends, playing with their children. Our parents did warn us about kidnappers, and about accepting candy or a ride from a stranger; but apart from that, our free time was our own and we did some dangerous things.

I was always cooking up mischief and sometimes getting Randy, or one of the neighbors, to go along with my schemes—some of which, in hindsight, bordered on petty crime. I remember stealing the Tarvers' candy jar and then hiding in the weeds on the vacant lot between our house and Uncle David's when Mother came looking for me, switch in hand. Another time, I led Pam Tarver and Mark Wright, another playmate, to a farm three blocks from our house (out of the approved "roaming range") to collect goose eggs. My mother once asked, in exasperation, "Why can't you be more like Pam?". I was not sure which one of my friends she was comparing me to, but I knew exactly what she meant.

Perhaps because I was so mischievous, my mother often allowed me to go (or maybe sent me) to the home of my paternal grandparents, Wyatt Langford and Nettie Estelle Horne Hester, where I transformed myself into an angel. Grandmother Hester adored me and loved having me—the little girl she always wanted—at the two-story frame house my grandfather had built for the family in 1928. It had four bedrooms, two on the main floor for my grandparents and my grandmother's spinster sister, who lived with them, and two upstairs where their three sons, Ross, Carl, and David had slept. This house had been dedicated by the pastor of First Presbyterian Church, Dr. Jack Lewis, "to the glory and service of the Lord".

During my visits, Grandmother instructed me on the Catechism and the family tree, and I became proficient at both. She baked bread weekly and taught me how to knead the dough. She taught me to embroider and crochet, and how to use her sewing machine. We took homemade bread or cookies, or sometimes roses or dahlias cut from her garden, to her friends in the neighborhood, and they would give her a squash, or a bag of green beans or okra, or a jar of homemade jelly in exchange. She liked making these social calls to show me off, but also used them to coach me on my manners.

Grandmother began preparing a full farmhouse dinner each day around eleven o'clock—fried chicken or meatloaf or ham—and we listened to Paul Harvey tell "the rest of the story" on the kitchen radio while we cooked. Granddaddy came home from Hester's Office Furniture and Supply Store, the business he started the same year he built the house, about twelve-thirty, and went directly to either his Bible or his hymnal, teaching me a Psalm or a song before we sat down to eat. Then Grandmother and I would retire to the two single beds in their room. She read the paper until she fell asleep, and I looked at books. I would usually fall asleep too; in the summertime, with only the swamp cooler upstairs, it was too hot to do anything else. Granddaddy took his nap in his recliner in the living room, with a baseball game on the radio at low volume, before returning to work until after dark.

My great-aunt, May Horne, was legally blind, and wore a green plastic visor, the kind stereotypically associated with old-time accountants and copy editors. She would invite me into her bedroom with the offer of a sugar-coated lemon drop and proceed to talk to me about the "blood of the Lamb." This, I learned years later, drove my mother crazy, but she felt helpless to intervene. Aunt May played Tennessee Ernie Ford, whose genre was mostly gospel hymns, but also country, including *Sixteen Tons*, a song I liked. May received recorded music, books, and sermons from the National Library Service for Blind Adults, of which the Texas State Library was a participant. Later, when I could, I read to her, mostly from the Bible, as did my father's cousin, Tom Hester. A framed photograph of evangelist Billy Graham, with his wife and children, sat on May's dresser, and it was years before I realized they were not members of our extended family.

On days when going to my grandparents' house was not an option (mostly due to my grandmother's extensive volunteer work as president of the Women of the Church for El Paso Presbytery), my father might take me downtown, where he was a pressman in the print shop at Hester's. I was allowed to choose any supplies I wanted to set up my own office on the second floor, in the furniture showroom. From an early age I had a desk equipped with pen, pencil, paper, stapler, paper clips, tape, and scissors. I would wander back to the print shop from time to time and ask Daddy for coins to put in the Coke and candy machines in the break room. One of the secretaries would take me to the lunch counter at Dunlap's Department Store down the street. I felt like a real little executive.

The September before I turned six, my mother enrolled me in Mrs. Cunningham's Kindergarten— a half-day program held in a garage—where I learned to read and write. The following September, during the first week of first grade (which I had excitedly begun with my friends Pam Cass and Pam Tarver) at Hodges Elementary School, I was escorted out of my classroom and into a second grade one, pre-sumably because of my ability to read *Dick and Jane*. My new class-mates made fun of me because all I had for lunch was a banana and three cents, for milk; first graders were not yet staying for a full day of school, and that was to have been my snack. I did not adjust well, and spent too much time looking out the window and daydreaming that year. Every six weeks I received a check mark, indicating improvement needed, in the "Works without wasting time" box on my report card.

The following year, we moved to a new house in a new neighbor-hood, and Uncle Eldon and his wife, Mary Reese Hobbs, and their growing family bought the house he had helped to build. I began third grade at Bayless Elementary School. The thirteen hundred block of Fifty-ninth Street was lined with new three-bedroom ranch style houses like ours, and I could walk to Bayless, and later to Atkins Junior High. My siblings and I made friends with everyone on the block, including the Thorns, who had four daughters. Jenny, the old-est, was two years older than I and one grade ahead of me in school. Her father, the Reverend William Thorn, was my Aunt May's pastor at Calvary Baptist Church.

Jenny was as mischievous as I. One day, that first year at Bayless, my father dropped us off at school, but instead of going into the build-ing we turned around and walked toward home. We left our book bags in a vacant house we planned to return to, and made our way to a convenience store located on the Tahoka Circle on the southeast outskirts of town. There we spent our lunch money on candy, chips, and soda pop. The school principal, Mr. Jackson, had seen us leave and immediately called our parents. It wasn't long before my mother and Jenny's father found us. I remember him saying to his daughter: "You'd better enjoy that Coke, because it's the last one you're going to have for a long time." I assume that back home she was scolded and spanked, as I was.

The Thorns always invited me to attend church with them on Wednesday and Sunday nights; they knew I was at my own church on Sunday morning. I especially enjoyed being part of the Girls' Auxiliary, corollary to the boys' Royal Ambassadors—essentially, training to become a missionary—which I was sure I wanted to do. I was fascinated with the baptismal pool in the sanctuary, where converts were submerged after they accepted Jesus during the alter call. I found myself wanting to walk down the aisle as the choir sang *Just as I Am*, wanting to commit myself to Jesus over and over, and try to be a better girl. But being Presbyterian, I was baptized as an infant, and knew we believed in one baptism, so I never did. Sometimes I saw Aunt May at Calvary, and sometimes I spoke to her; at other times I did not, taking advantage of her blindness.

In the spring of 1959, toward the end of my fourth-grade year, Mother and I were shelling black-eyed peas with her mother and her younger sister, Julia, in Grandmother Hobbs's kitchen, when Mother revealed some exciting but disturbing news. She was expecting a fifth child, and our family was moving to Phoenix. My parents owned a yellow Rambler station wagon, which had been stolen the past winter and located by police in Arizona. Mother and Daddy flew out to claim the car, during which time they fell in love with the desert—the winter warmth, the palm trees, and the Spanish-style estates with pools and citrus groves. My parents had met at Mo-Ranch, a Presbyterian camp and conference center located in the Texas Hill Country, and after marrying shortly thereafter, in May of 1948, begun their family. They had probably not had a vacation alone since.

Just prior to the time of Mother's revelation, my father had started a new business, Caprock Business Forms; but he had a partner, Dick Crandall, who was willing to carry on in his absence. After getting confirmation of a pressman job in Phoenix, finding renters for our house in Lubbock, and saying a tearful goodbye to their parents, my father and my expectant mother, my three siblings and I, and our dog drove from Lubbock to Phoenix in the Rambler. Summer in Phoenix was beyond warm, and our plain rental house had no palm trees or pool, but this was an adventure, and we embraced it. The poor dog, whose name I cannot remember, went missing shortly after our arrival, and we visited the pound daily for two weeks before resigning ourselves to our loss. My youngest brother, Jeffrey Wyatt, was born on October 2, 1959, the only one in my family born outside of Texas.

I matured during my fifth-grade year, helping to care for the baby, coming directly home from school to hang diapers on the clothesline, working with Mother to prepare dinner, and doing the dishes afterward. I was successful in school. It was a chance to catch up from the lost year of social and emotional development, in a new environment. On Saturdays, my father took the four of us and the neighbor kids to the mountain parks around Phoenix and cooked breakfast for us on a camp stove, and on Sunday mornings he took us downtown to First Presbyterian Church. Mother typically stayed home with the baby.

Halfway through our time in Arizona, my parents learned the business they had started was not going well in Daddy's absence. Their choices were limited—let it go, or return to Lubbock, which they decided to do. We returned home after a year; Daddy had received fifty-two paychecks in Phoenix.

Daddy worked hard to turn things around in Lubbock, and with his excellent business and people skills, eventually built one of the most successful business forms manufacturing businesses in the Southwest. Even with the pressure of supporting our family of seven, and as many as forty-five employees and their families, my father once told me he never worried about money. He was a man of remarkable faith.

During the summers of Caprock's early years, my mother and Grandmother Hobbs would take the five of us, and Aunt Julia and Uncle Gerry—Mother's little brother, who was in the same grade as I—to a small rustic cabin in Pecos, New Mexico, owned by two of my father's aunts. Along the route Mother would stop in to visit printers in Albuquerque and Santa Fe, promoting business and collecting overdue accounts. As we grew older, she became increasingly involved in the business and took accounting courses at Texas Tech to enhance her value to it. Mother was an integral part of the success of Caprock Business Forms.

All of us worked for Caprock at different times while growing up, but it was my brother, Steve, who devoted his career to its success. After graduating from Austin College, where he met Olive Munholland Montgomery, a southern belle from Monroe, Louisiana working on her Master of Education degree, Steve began a promising career with the Travelers Insurance Companies. He worked for them first in Dallas and, after he and Olive married August 1, 1981, in Lubbock. But when asked to move from Lubbock to El Paso, he declined, and returned to Caprock. He took over the business as president in 1994. Caprock turned sixty in 2018, the same year Steve negotiated the sale of its name and customer base to Ennis Business Forms, at which point we rebranded our company as Hestco. The real estate was sold in September of 2021, just after Daddy died, to a developer, who wanted to keep one of the old printing presses in recognition of the property's history. We have heard that the city plans to designate the commercial redevelopment of our land and its surroundings *The Press District* which, if true, will be a fitting legacy.

Growing up in my family was fun and a little chaotic, with five children, our friends, and various dogs, cats, birds, gerbils and even snakes in the mix. Christmas was an especially fun time. We baked and decorated countless sugar cookies. We sprayed trees and reindeer and angels on the windows with fake snow. We made homemade paper chains and popcorn and cranberry garlands for the tree, which we usually bought on the way home from church in early December. Mother favored silver tinsel "icicles" and insisted we hang them one at a time—not throw them—on the branches. Each child opened one gift from our parents on Christmas Eve, typically a pair of pajamas, after a fun evening at my Hester grandparents' home with my cousins, Mel, Tina, and Karen, and their parents. After we went to bed and the younger children fell asleep, I lay awake listening to my parents laughing and assembling our toys. They got a little tipsy on Christmas Eve. Our Santa Claus gifts were left unwrapped, arranged in individual gleaming piles under the tree, one for each child, our stockings draped over them, to be attacked early Christmas morning. Later that day we would go to my Hobbs grandparents' home for more presents, and dinner.

The tree came down before we returned to school, and joined other Christmas trees we collected from the alleys around our house in becoming a fort in our backyard. During the tree gathering expedition of my sixth-grade year, some neighborhood kids and I discovered pornography. We were in the alley behind the home of our across-the-street neighbors, and under their discarded tree sat stacks of *Penthouse* and *Hustler* magazines. We could not help but look at them. The couple who lived in the house were older than my parents, very nice and very normal, with two sons and a daughter, whose wedding my youngest brother was ring-bearer in. I later learned the husband, who was nicknamed "Red", was involved in all manner of criminal activity—gambling, bootlegging (Lubbock was "dry"), and prostitution. He eventually went to Leavenworth Prison, where he died of a heart attack, my mother in disbelief of his guilt to the end.

That same Christmas vacation, my brother Randy took an interest in my playing the piano and asked me to show him how. I had started taking lessons from a woman named Bonnie before we moved to Phoenix and resumed them on our return. I was not very good and did not like to practice but loved being awarded the small white busts of famous composers after participating in a recital. I pointed out "Middle C" to Randy, and played a scale or two, then found one of my primary books and helped him with the fingering. By the end of our break, my brother had mastered every book in my collection. As I remember it, my parents explained there was only enough money for one of us to take music lessons, and Randy obviously had a gift. My brother replaced me at the piano bench.

Two years later, Bonnie told my parents she had taught Randy all she could and advised them to find a more advanced teacher. He continued to play and to compose music. While obtaining his degree in mechanical engineering at Texas Tech, after having attended both the University of California at Berkley and St. John's College in Annapolis, Maryland, Randy disassembled and rebuilt a piano. In 1985, he met Elenita Buenaventura, a petite Filipina woman, in a music theory class at Tech. Lyn, as she is known, was working on a Master of Music Performance degree. Her father, Alfredo Buenaventura, was a classical composer and orchestra conductor in Manila. Randy and Lyn were married in Pampa, Texas, where she had lived with her uncle, a physician, on July 19, 1986. Randy worked for many years as plant manager for Caprock, continuing to play classical pieces on his Yamaha concert grand piano, and eventually teaching himself to play violin.

After realigning the music lessons, my parents went to work realigning my bite. I had terrible buck teeth, and my father's dentist cousin referred us to an orthodontist, Dr. R., who brought me to tears on numerous occasions, and who we later learned was an abusive spouse. I saw him regularly from sixth grade through tenth, when my braces finally came off. Dr. R. presented my extreme case at a national dental convention, a fact my father reminded me of often over the years. My treatment was such a financial sacrifice for my parents that I never told them how cruel the man had been to me.

Like most of my generation, I remember where I was when I learned that John F. Kennedy had been assassinated. I assisted in the Atkins school office two periods a week, and during one of those, on the morning of Friday, November 21, 1963, my social studies teacher walked out of the principal's office with tears in his eyes. Soon, an announcement came over the PA system— the President of the United States had been shot and killed in Dallas. Everyone wept. That night, my family and my best friend, Phyllis Minton (now Phyllis Shamoon and still my best friend) went out to dinner at El Charro, still in shock. We were Republicans, among the many who had feared having a Catholic as president (a fear that seems ridiculous to me now), but we were grief-stricken.

Most of our traditional Friday night dinners out were at Furr's Cafeteria, and in high school I would often drive myself there to meet my family before returning home to go out on a date. One such night, during my sophomore year, I hurried home to change into an elegant new ice-blue silver lame skirt and top for a dance I had been invited to attend with an upperclassman, only to realize the gold studs I was wearing clashed with my outfit. I had recently had my ears pierced, among the first in my class to do so, emulating a friend, Janet (now Meredith) Abbey, whose cool older sister was a trend setter at Monterey High School, which we attended. These gold studs were to have remained in my ears for another week, but I quickly decided to replace them early. I removed the first one, confident I could insert a pearl stud in its place. I could not. My family returned home minutes before my date arrived, and my father was able—with difficulty—to insert a needle through the back of my ear and guide the pearl stud through from the front. Neither of us realized our mistake until it was too late, and I went to the dance with a gold stud in one ear and a pearl one in the other.

That outfit was one of only a few that were purchased. Mother made most of my clothes, and her own and my sister's too; she was an expert seamstress. After I learned to sew myself, in sixth grade, my wardrobe became a joint project. I bought *Ingenue, Glamour, Mademoiselle,* and *Vogue*—tearing out pictures and looking for fabric—and Mother flipped through pattern books looking for one we could alter to duplicate the creation I had in mind. In a brief memoir, Mother writes about "the hectic rush of trying to finish some new dress before Sherry's date arrived—even finishing <u>after</u> he arrived!" I made dresses and skirts, a madras matched-plaid blazer and, in 1964, a fully lined street length Courrèges-style wool coat with bound buttonholes, but my sewing never matched the standard of perfection my mother's achieved.

In the fall of our junior year, Phyllis and I enrolled in "charm school", a series of classes taught at Dunlap's Department Store by our friend Sherron Schmidt's elegant mother, Martha. The two of us and Sherron were the only students, and we received personalized attention on the topics of fashion, make-up, hairstyles, nutrition, poise, and etiquette. The classes were held after school, and by the time they were over we were famished. We would stop at Sparkman's Bakery on the way home for a bag of powdered-sugar coated pecan sandies, completely ignoring Martha's guidelines for maintaining a slim figure.

In junior high, and continuing into high school, I was placed in honors English and math classes. My primary interest—besides boys—was public speaking, and I participated in extemporaneous speech, oral interpretation, and debate—traveling by bus with other students and our teacher sponsors to competitions around West Texas, occasionally winning in my category. I also performed in school plays but was most often cast as understudy to Alice Cochran, a beautiful and funny girl from a wealthy family. Two other girls in our drama class, Peggy Sheffield and Rhonda Lamoreaux, were the younger sisters of women I remain friends with today. These three actresses have all passed on, and I cherish the memories of our fun times together.

From the time I entered my teens, I was eager to move from Lubbock in search of a bigger world. But I did not know how to negotiate that path and had no clear vision for my future. My father talked to me about attending his alma mater, Austin College, in Sherman, Texas, near Dallas, an excellent liberal arts college affiliated with the Presbyterian Church, but he never took me there to visit. Instead of focusing on college preparation, I allowed my relationship with my boyfriend, Bill Fisher, who I had met in a debate class and who was now enrolled at Tech, to become too serious. By the spring of my senior year most of my friends had made plans to enter Tech in the fall, and I had become pregnant. When I told my mother, she said, "Go tell your father." When I told my father, he said, "We'd better call Clem."

After tearfully resigning herself to the situation, Mother planned a lovely wedding and reception. My friends inserted a generous bridal shower into the flurry of graduation parties. Bill and I were married on May 31, 1967, at Grace Presbyterian Church—chosen for its beautiful chapel with stained-glass windows—where my Hobbs grandparents were long-time members. Phyllis was my bridesmaid, and our pastor, the Reverend Clement Lambreth, officiated. Bill was two months shy of twenty; I was seventeen years and five months old. We took a short honeymoon, then set up housekeeping in a two-bedroom duplex located fifteen blocks south of the Tech campus.

Bill was a salesman for a men's clothier, Malouf's, full-time during the summer and part-time during the school year. My recent summer jobs at Caprock were too physically strenuous for my condition, so Uncle David introduced me to one of his former classmates who worked in administration at Tech. I was hired to sort incoming college mail, which I did alone in a remote location on the edge of the campus. The huge bags of mail delivered to me each morning included recommendations addressed to fraternity and sorority houses for incoming freshmen who hoped to pledge that fall. I would sometimes hold the sheer, handwritten envelopes up to the light to see if I could read their contents. I alternated between envy of my friends who were preparing to enter college and go through rush, and excitement about my growing belly and the new life it held.

This job also became too strenuous; the mailbags were heavy. Ann Fisher, my mother-in-law, had worked her husband through dental school years earlier. She suggested that I could make more money in a professional office, if I were to learn some new skills. I had purposely avoided typing classes in high school because I did not want to become a secretary; though, ironically, my grandfather's business sold more typewriters than any other distributer in the area. Now, reluctantly, I enrolled in Draughon's Business College, located in an upstairs office space between Hester's Office Furniture and Supplies, and Hester's Office Machines. Sitting for hours was miserable, and the ceiling fans overhead just seemed to move the hot air around, but I did learn to type. I also reached a tipping point.

I asked my parents over to our small apartment on a Sunday afternoon in late August. I told them I knew I had made mistakes but was committed to working my way through them. I asked if they would pay for my college and help with childcare—both of which they eagerly agreed to do. The next week, I matriculated at Texas Tech, and in September began attending classes, taking just six hours that first semester. In the first page of an autograph book my mother gave me for my ninth birthday she had written, "Honey, you are a sweet and pretty little girl, and I am proud of you. Here's wishing you the best of everything in life and remember—I'll always be standing by." My life would not be what it is today without the steadfast support of my parents.

Three months later, on Thanksgiving Day, I was standing in the kitchen rolling out a pie crust, when I began to feel pressure in my lower abdomen. I called my mother, who was hosting both sides of the family for dinner, to ask if she thought it would be okay for me to take some Milk of Magnesia for what I assumed was constipation. She instructed me to call my doctor, who instructed me to meet him at the hospital. I gave birth to Boyd Wyatt Fisher at 1:28 p.m. that day, November twenty-third. Ironically, my uncle, Gerry Hobbs, a handsome linebacker and offensive guard at Lubbock High School, who had also graduated the past spring and recently married his high school sweetheart, head majorette Kay Evans, had a son the following day. David Paul Hobbs, my cousin, was born November 24, 1967. Grandmother Hobbs had been mortified that her youngest child and her oldest grandchild were both expecting before marriage. But she showered those little boys with love when they arrived.

Bo was a colicky baby, crying through the night unless being held, and it was impossible for me to sleep. Most fathers then did not take the active parenting role they do today. Our mothers took turns spending the night for a few weeks until we hired a nurse to come in. I completed my final exams and immediately enrolled in two more classes. I feared if I took even one semester off from school, I might lose my momentum and fail to graduate.

Bo's colic subsided, and parenting became fun. Once I got past the basic freshman courses and into my major, which was speech, school also became fun. I worked part-time in the office at Caprock, and then at Margaret's, an upscale women's clothing store in Lubbock, while my grandparents cared for Bo. Bill continued at Malouf's. We had an active social life, getting together regularly with several couples, Steve and Teri (Sudderth) Maeker and Bill and Jane (Sheffield) Byrd in particular, who had been at Monterey with us and were now at Tech. Phyllis had started college at West Texas State in Canyon, but came home often to visit her parents, me, and Bo, who she teased, saying "I'd rather be dead than red on the head." She later transferred to and graduated from Tech.

It's hard to say when and why my marriage started to unravel. To state the obvious, Bill and I were too young to be married. But many such marriages have survived and thrived (though neither of the aforementioned). We grew apart rather than growing together. My chosen major required too many outside engagements, so I switched to sociology, which tends to attract a more liberal student. Bill was enrolled in the College of Business Administration. The late 1960's was the era of Viet Nam War protests, the evolution of a more radical contingent of the Civil Rights movement, and the emerging Women's Movement—each of which reignited my earlier desire to escape my conservative surroundings. My interest and restrained involvement in these were, I'm sure, perceived as a threat to our marriage—which, in fact, they were. Bill and I divorced in 1970, and I began plotting my move to Austin and my transfer to the University of Texas, much to the distress of my parents and grandparents, and the Fishers.

Bo and I arrived in Austin the evening of January 1, 1971, the day after my twenty-first birthday. The Longhorns had been defeated that afternoon in the Cotton Bowl by the Fighting Irish of Notre Dame, and the mood was somber. I drove a Volvo sedan, and my parents pulled a U-haul containing my furniture—two single beds, one of which would double by day as a sofa, a Pier 1 wicker table, four ladder-back chairs, a chest of drawers, a sewing machine cabinet containing the Singer that had been my grandmother's and then my mother's, its matching stool, and a couple of cubes that would serve as a coffee table. I'll never forget my feelings of fear and elation as my parents drove away that same night, headed south on Interstate-35 for a visit with Mother's sister, Mary, and her husband, Max, in San Antonio.

Austin was everything I had imagined, and more. The campus is bordered to the south by Martin Luther King (then 19th Street) with the state capital beyond, and to the north by 26th Street, with the beautiful and serene Austin Seminary campus beyond. Guadalupe Street runs along the west side of the campus, and at that time was a buzzing amalgam of students, hippies, anti-war protesters, and demonstrators of various ilk, as was the historic campus itself. I wanted to fit into this counterculture, but my attempt at alternative dress more resembled a stylish ethnic look. A small group of friends from Lubbock, including a first-year law student named Tom Caldwell, who I had met at a holiday party just before moving, welcomed me to town. Tom offered to show me around and we visited Schultz's Beer Garden, where I had been instructed by my uncles—Carl, a UT graduate himself, and David—to lift a stein to them, and the Split Rail, where I fell in love with a band called Freda and the Firedogs, led by Marcia Ball, now of the Marcia Ball Band, who I'm still in love with.

My first three orders of business were to arrange for childcare, enroll in classes, and find a job—each of which went more smoothly than I had dared hope for. I dated a few men, including a friend of a friend who had a son Bo's age, but soon became Tom's constant companion. During the summer between graduation from Texas Tech University and entry into the University of Texas School of Law, Tom had traveled with a group of friends to Europe, using Frommer's

Europe on Five Dollars a Day. He had come back so thin that when he reported to the draft board for service in Viet Nam he was rejected, to his delight and relief. Tom had a keen sense of humor, an appreciation for art, literature and classical music, and a love of travel. Even though we had known each other a short time and I had not yet processed the failure of my first marriage, we decided to wed, in the fall of 1971, at the Travis County Courthouse. The Justice of the Peace was named Buck Smith.

Grandmother Hester wrote to me faithfully during the two and a half years I lived in Austin. Her letters were a blend of encouragement, family news, and admonishment to join a church. I visited University Presbyterian, located a block from the UT campus, where my father's cousin, Goldia Hester, was the long-time Clerk of Session, but it was just too easy to find other fun things to do on Sunday mornings, even though I have always felt a nagging sense of emptiness when I am not in worship on the first day of the week.

Early in 1972, having just turned twenty-two, I discovered I was pregnant again, even though I was using the birth control provided me by the university's student health clinic. This was devastating news, even though I loved my husband and, of course, my son. Graduation was in sight—just a year to go—but I found it difficult to visualize how I could continue to work, care for a four-year-old *and* a baby, and complete my degree. I had joined the local chapter of the National Women's Political Caucus, founded by Gloria Steinem in 1971. Sarah Weddington, an Austin attorney who would soon argue *Roe v. Wade* before the Supreme Court, was a frequent meeting attendee, and the discussion often centered around women's right to reproductive freedom, so I was familiar with my limited options.

Abortion was not legal in Texas but could be obtained in California. Tom agreed with my decision, and we drove to Los Angeles for me to have the surgical procedure. The clinic was immaculate, and the staff was kind. When we next visited our parents, we shared the choice we had made, and they were accepting and supportive, though I suspect the Caldwells hid their grief. Tom's mother said something, intended as comfort, about the population explosion, referencing a 1968 book by Paul Ehrlich titled *The Population Bomb*, written to encourage a lower birth rate, among other actions, to alleviate world hunger and stress on the planet. But my decision was based solely on my desire to live my life without the added responsibility of another child at that time, a right I continue to advocate for women today.

I graduated with a Bachelor of Arts degree in sociology in December of 1972, just before turning twenty-three. My parents, who were now divorced, came to Austin for my ceremony the following May, and in hindsight I wish we had attended it. Instead, I suggested we all attend Tom's graduation from law school, being held concurrently. What mattered most to me at the time was not walking across a stage but having a diploma in my hands.

We moved to San Antonio in the summer of 1973, and Tom reported to work for the three justices at the Court of Civil Appeals, located near the historic River Walk. We purchased an older home at 306 Thorman Place, located a few miles north of downtown near a bus route Tom would travel daily, and within easy walking distance of Brackenridge Park, with its zoo and botanic gardens. The purchase price was $18,500; the down payment came from a Prudential Life Insurance policy my parents had bought when I was a child that endowed for $2,000 on my twenty-first birthday. Our furnishings were meager, but our next-door neighbor was an antiques dealer, and she generously provided an upholstered sofa and two chairs that were not the quality she desired to sell, but which were perfectly adequate for our needs. Soon after we moved, there were several break-ins involving sexual assaults in our area, and we decided we needed a dog. A family down the street had a litter of German shepherds. We selected a female, and I named her Germaine, after Germaine Greer, feminist author of *The Female Eunuch*.

I looked for a job doing social work, but one interview at the Department of Human Services convinced me this was not my calling. I wanted to help people, but I also wanted to make money commensurate with my willingness to work hard, and I needed a flexible schedule for combining parenting and career. When the opportunity arose, I went to work as an insurance agent for a Dallas-based company, Fidelity Union Life, on straight commission, and committed myself to helping other young women become more financially knowledgeable and economically secure.

As we explored our new neighborhood, we discovered a large, rambling two-story house a few blocks south of ours, with children playing on the grounds and a sign that read "The New Age School". After a series of interviews, I enrolled Bo in this independent school, a hybrid blend of Montessori, Waldorf, and other non-traditional learning, where he completed the equivalent of kindergarten and first grade.

One of the school parents I became friends with belonged to the local chapter of the National Organization for Women. I joined the diverse group, which included St. Mary's Law School students, UT Health Sciences Center interns and residents, working professionals, and stay-at-home moms. These women were my community for the next two years. We met monthly to strategize and socialize. We attended the National NOW Conference together in Houston in 1974 to hone our skills at social and political activism. We hosted Gloria Steinem on a visit she and Sissy Farenthold made to our city in their campaign to garner support for Texas' ratification of the Equal Rights Amendment. In addition to being friends and colleagues, many of these women became my clients, and they introduced me to other women—and to their husbands—who became clients, too. My insurance practice was thriving.

Mary Alice and Max Allen, Mother's younger sister and her husband, lived less than ten miles north of us in Windcrest, a suburb of San Antonio. They had two adopted children, Melanie and Mark—unrelated by birth to each other—just a little older than Bo, and we were often in their home, where Max's mother, Marguerite, also lived. Mary was a combination of big sister and second mother to me, and like another grandmother to Bo. Max, an attorney who had also attended UT for both undergraduate studies and law school, enjoyed sailing and often took Tom out in his boat on Canyon Lake. Mary and Max had a very traditional marriage; in fact, he typified what I secretly referred to as a "male chauvinist". Max and I sparred verbally over my feminist beliefs and the activities I was involved in, but I tried not to let him get under my skin, because he and Mary were both so good to me and my family. I know he would beam with pride over what his daughter, Melanie Allen Kirk, has accomplished as founding and managing partner of one of the top accounting firms in San Antonio and mentor to many through the National Association of Women Business Owners. Melanie and her brother are the cousins I am closest to on my mother's side of the family. Mark shared with me recently some of the details he and Mel have learned regarding the circumstances of their births. He is convinced that, had abortion been legal in Texas at the time, neither he nor Melanie would be alive today. I must admit, this gives me pause, as I love them both so dearly.

By 1975, Tom was ready to move on and began to look for a job that combined his law degree and his recently completed masters degree in tax accounting. He narrowed his choices to firms in Portland, Seattle, and Denver. An avid skier, he chose Colorado. We sold our house for a small profit and moved in August, renting a house seven miles south of Castle Rock. After a trip to Yellowstone National Park, Tom reported to Haskins & Sells in downtown Denver, Bo started second grade at Castle Rock Elementary, and I began work at the Denver office of Fidelity Union. We bought new furniture and reciprocated in entertaining several couples that had feted us during Tom's recruiting process. Colorado's fall colors were beautiful, and the view of Pike's Peak from our deck was stunning, but we had a rude awakening when winter set in and we had to plow not only our driveway, but the road from the end of our driveway to the county road. I feel ashamed to admit how quickly I despaired, leaving my husband and running back to Texas, with Bo, this time to a position in the Dallas home office of the insurance company I represented.

By the next summer, Tom had moved into the Pebble Creek Apartments in southwest Denver, and I had moved back in with him. Bo went to live with Bill and his wife, Mary Ann, entering third grade in Houston. The real estate market in Denver was crazy in 1977, with offers being made on homes the prospective buyers had not even seen the inside of, but we managed to secure a three-bedroom ranch-style home on South University in the Southern Hills neighborhood, again on a bus route Tom could use to get to his downtown office.

Tom had yet to complete all four sections of the CPA exam, and took a review course held at Trinity Methodist Church, located at Broadway and Eighteenth Avenue. He thought the church was beautiful and suggested we visit there on a Sunday, which we did. We were close to joining Trinity when Tom went on a weekend outing with some of his work associates and I decided to visit Central Presbyterian Church, located at Seventeenth Avenue and Sherman Street. The pastor, Dr. James Emerson, who went on to become president of San Francisco Theological Seminary, and his wife Margaret (who everyone called "Migs"), were presenting a dialogue from the pulpit. Not having done any homework before visiting, I thought the church had a female pastor, and I was hooked. The liturgy and the hymns were familiar to me, and the sanctuary, designed in 1860 by Frank Edbrooke—architect of the Brown Palace—was majestic. Tom also liked Jim and Migs, who lived in our Southern Hills neighborhood and often invited church members to their home for food, wine, and conversation. We joined the church in the fall of 1977. (I am pleased to write that the church has had multiple female pastors since then, including the Reverend Dr. Louise Westfall, who married Lauren and Alex on June 18, 2017, and who baptized Stella on January 23, 2021. But those things come later.)

In 1978, I moved from Fidelity Union to Home Life of New York, a company more suited to providing the professional service I desired to offer my clients. I obtained my Chartered Life Underwriter designation in 1980, offered by The American College, and then the more advanced Chartered Financial Consultant designation, both of which I hold today. Eventually, with the latter, I was able to challenge the Certified Financial Planner exam in 1990 and have continuously renewed my license by fulfilling the ongoing educational requirements.

The capacity of my clientele and the quality of referrals from other professionals grew with these credentials, and when I retired from my practice at age sixty, it was an asset. It was a tremendous privilege to assist others in achieving their financial goals. More than ten years later, I still get the occasional note, email, or call from former clients thanking me for the comfortable retirement they are enjoying, or for the extra encouragement to purchase a life or disability insurance policy. One woman, who is prominent in Denver's non-profit community, recently introduced me to her daughter at a fundraiser as "the person who made it possible for you to attend any college you wanted". I reminded them both it was their commitment and sacrifice that was responsible for their success; I merely guided the process.

During my thirty-seven years in insurance and financial services, I represented multiple companies, most of which have different names today. The world of financial services has morphed and changed, but a continuing benefit to a career in financial planning is having access to the tools and information needed to create financial independence for oneself, and I would encourage any aspiring young person to consider it. Early on, I had a paperweight on my desk that read, "In order to be successful a career woman must look like a woman, act like a lady, think like a man, and work like a dog." I exchanged it mid-career for a small plaque that read, "It's my job to let people know who I am, and what I do well." I made duplicates of this one for each of my children.

I found it important to be involved in my professional and trade organizations and developed great respect for competitors representing other companies. My colleagues elected me president of the Denver Association of Life Underwriters, (now the Denver chapter of the National Association of Insurance and Financial Advisors), and the Rocky Mountain Chapter of CLU and ChFC, now the Society of Financial Service Professionals. I was active in the Denver Estate Planning Council, and taught insurance and estate planning classes for the Life Underwriter Training Council and for the CFP certification program at Metropolitan State University. Each of these experiences provided a new opportunity for personal and professional growth. They are also responsible for some of my most enduring friendships— the Nettings, the Millimans, the Morens, and the Persons.

I relied heavily on existing clients for introductions to new prospective clients, and would typically ask a series of questions to prompt their thinking: "Who do you know who just got married, had a baby, bought a house, started a business?" Sometime in the fall of 1983, I was referred to "a successful young architect who just started his own practice, and probably needs to buy disability insurance." I tried never to assume a person's needs before conducting a comprehensive fact-finding interview, and invited Andy Kenney to lunch at The Chrysler, located above The Tattered Cover in Cherry Creek, for an introductory meeting. When the subject of disability insurance did eventually come around, he was eager to pursue it, as both of his parents and his three older siblings had experienced health issues. I could not have foreseen then that we would be married, that he would one day suffer a stroke, and that the disability policy I sold him would protect the financial success we achieved together over a period of thirty years.

Tom and I had recently purchased a house at 110 Krameria Street, in the Crestmoor Park neighborhood, from Central Presbyterian friends Kent and Glenda Winker, when they moved into the Denver Country Club neighborhood. The house was a split-level ranch that needed updating, and I bid on and won two hours with a decorating team at a silent charity auction. The consultation turned into a longer-term engagement, and then into a nightmare that created extreme tension between my husband and me. Andy offered to help us work our way through the renovation debacle, and he and I became close. He was married to a woman I knew and respected, but I learned that, for him, it was not a happy marriage.

Sadly, during our thirteen years together, Tom and I developed neither a level of intimacy and trust, nor a process for conflict resolution, to get us successfully through difficult times, including the one we were in. There is enough blame to go around for these failures, and I accept my share. Some may say Andy and I each broke up the other's marriage, but our marriages were—if not already broken—deeply fractured. Regardless, it is not easy for me to live with the knowledge my actions caused pain to other people. Andy and his wife separated early in 1984, and Tom and I separated that summer after a series of failed counseling sessions. A cache of tender letters from Tom's mother, whom I loved dearly, recently resurfaced, and reminded me of the ripple effects of divorce.

Andy rented a one-bedroom apartment on the second floor of the Washington Irving, a beautiful, old four-story building located at Tenth and Pennsylvania avenues and owned by Steve and Jo Culbertson, friends of mine at Central. Later, I rented a two-bedroom apartment on the third floor of the same building. A friend from my Junior League provisional class, Katharine Kunz Nanda, represented me in divorce proceedings that were finalized in December of 1984, gently stressing the importance of prioritizing good will over property. As those who have been through it know, divorce often involves a division of friends, some of whom feel they must choose sides. But I was surprised when Tom asked me which of us would get the church. He reasoned it would be awkward for both of us to attend, that I had the more outgoing personality and would find it easier to make new friends at a new church. I reluctantly agreed.

However, the Reverend John Wilcox, then the pastor at Central Presbyterian, stopped by my office in the Great-West Life Tower (located three blocks west of the church), in the spring of 1985, to encourage me back. He told me Tom was not attending worship and there was no reason for the church to lose both of us. I agreed to return, with Andy. Mary and Denny Linden, Fritz and Clarice Hill, John and Nancy Stamper, Gail and Ed Fisher, and the Winkers rushed to meet him and made us both feel welcome. I experienced no judgement, only grace, and joy at being back in my faith community.

These same friends invited us to take the place vacated by Joe and Elizabeth Rice, who had moved to South Carolina, in their bridge group, and together with another couple, Howard and Audrey Watters, we constituted what we all, for many years, referred to simply as the Bridge Group. This group of friends, including the Rices, has been an important part of our lives for many years, though four have passed on.

In August of 1985, Bo totaled my car. He was distraught in the knowledge that excess speed and loud music had contributed to an accident, involving a mother and her baby, that could have been far more serious than it was. He enrolled in a defensive driving class and is an excellent driver today. But I had to replace my car, and once Bo returned to Houston for school, I set aside the next Saturday for a shopping expedition. Andy went with me. He has always loved cars and shopping for cars, and when a used Mercedes he had identified turned out not to be right for me, he bought it for himself. (I ended up leasing a new Cadillac Eldorado.)

As we discussed our concern about parking two luxury vehicles in the alley behind the Washington Irving, we passed an open house event for a new condominium development, Cedar Court, located at 221 South Garfield, in Cherry Creek. We toured the model units and decided—on the spot—to purchase one. A home under contract and two new cars called for celebration, so we sat on the patio at Rick's Café (now Chopper's Sports Grill), just two blocks north of our new condo, and drank champagne. It was here we decided to set a wedding date: December 21, 1985.

The Book of Order of the Presbyterian Church (USA) requires pastors to counsel any couple whose marriage they will officiate. The counseling we received from John Wilcox involved each of us making two lists, "I want for us…", and "I need from you…". We still have our lists, written on now faded sheets from a yellow legal pad, and we review them regularly, usually on our anniversary. We have each grown and changed in the thirty-seven years since we wrote them, but, unlike in our previous marriages, we have been laser-focused on our mutual goals throughout that growth and change. These lists have been our roadmap for the life we have made together.

The sanctuary of Central Presbyterian Church is decorated every year during Advent, in anticipation of Christmas, and in 1985, the

Stampers oversaw the effort. They added a new feature that year to the garlands of fresh greenery that draped the chancel—a huge evergreen bell. I sent handwritten wedding invitations to our close friends and family members. There was a series of parties honoring us, given by the Winkers, the Hills, and the Culbertsons. Our dear friend Annette Beaird, now departed, hosted a rehearsal dinner in her home for my visiting family, Andy's parents, and the Bridge Group.

The wedding was at eleven o'clock in the morning, followed by a brunch reception at Trinity Grille, 1801 Broadway—in the space now occupied by La Loma—which we rented in its entirety. The Winkers were our attendants, and the men in the Bridge Group, all wearing Christmas ties, were ushers. Bo escorted me down the aisle. I wore a lightweight ecru wool suit with knee length skirt and peplum jacket. I had previously purchased the suit at Neiman Marcus in Dallas, and it was gently used; however, Dick Auer, owner of the upscale, fashion-forward Auer's in Cherry Creek, personally assisted me in selecting new accessories—hat, kid leather gloves, shoes, and handbag, which I carried again thirty-two years later at Lauren's wedding.

Andy and I took a two-week honeymoon in Santa Fe, accompanied by Bo, after which he returned to Houston to complete his senior year, and we returned to Denver to settle into our new home and get back to work. Andy had told me there were two tasks he would not perform—cleaning the cat box and hanging wallpaper. He did both. Buck, a flame-point Siamese, had accompanied me from South University Boulevard to Krameria Street, to the Washington Irving, to Cedar Court. He remained a member of the family until I became pregnant with Lauren a year later, when his cat-sense must have told him the affection he demanded and received would soon have to be shared. He engaged in a series of obnoxious behaviors that my morning sickness could not tolerate. We ran a classified ad, and the phone rang off the hook. Buck rode away in the arms of a delighted young boy without so much as a single "meow".

The church was such an important part of my life that it was not unusual to receive a call from John Wilcox, asking me to serve on a committee or to assist in worship. But when he called one Saturday evening early in 1987, it was to tell me that Tom Caldwell had been diagnosed with cancer; John wanted me to know prior to announcing this prayer concern the following morning. It was devastating news that cast a pall over an otherwise joy-filled time in my life. Ralph Thomas Caldwell died on November fifteenth of that same year at the age of thirty-nine, an excruciating loss for his family and friends.

Lauren was born August 20, 1987. By then, I was working in the home office of Great-West Life at its new U.S. headquarters in the Denver Tech Center, thanks to my good friend and colleague, Jan Netting, who was Manager of Advanced Sales. I worked until near my due date, and Bo came from Houston to be with us when the baby arrived. Again, I failed to recognize the signs of impending childbirth. After a day of sightseeing (a planetarium show, at the Museum of Nature and Science, and a tour of the Denver Mint) I slept through the night. The next morning, Andy took me for my now-weekly visit to Dr. Don Woodard, my obstetrician. He examined me briefly, then told me to sit down in the wheelchair the nurse had brought in, so I could be taken across the skybridge to Swedish Hospital. "Mrs. Kenney," he said, "you're in labor. When did your water break?" I remembered then how sweaty my cute maternity pantsuit had felt the previous day as Bo and I stood in line outside the Mint. The baby came at 3:41 p.m. Hours after Andy had gone home to sleep, Bo and his friend, John Anton, peeked their heads into my darkened hospital room. They had come from admiring the baby through the glass of the nursery window.

Because my two children are twenty years apart, having the second was like having a first, for the second time. Everything felt new to me, and, of course, Andy had never had a child. We behaved like nervous first-time parents. At night, we sat glued to the baby monitor, and when it emitted a muffled noise, we exclaimed together "It's the baby!", as though it could possibly be anything else. We crawled around on our hands and knees looking for things the baby might choke on. I remember one time finding a tiny plastic garment tag and holding it up accusingly to Andy, who was smitten by his little daughter. When he came home from work each night, he insisted on taking her into his arms, ignoring my admonition to first remove his necktie, which never looked the same after dry-cleaning.

My best friend, Phyllis, and her husband, Ellis, had their first and only child, Annie Michelle Shamoon, six weeks after we had Lauren. We exchanged parenting stories by phone and flew back and forth to visit each other so that our girls could get to know each other. Once, in Dallas, Phyllis and I discovered the girls had taken their crayons into Annie's bedroom and proceeded to color the walls. I was horrified and embarrassed, but Phyllis calmly stated she would call her painter the next day. We never learned whose idea this was, or if it was mutual spontaneity. I love Annie like another daughter and was thrilled when she became engaged to Chad Beitler, who she will marry on November 18, 2022, on Maui. We are very excited to attend.

Andy and I became friends with other families at our church who had young children. Coincidentally, most of the dads were architects. Some of the moms, including me, worked, but most were taking time off to parent. Several of them, including our associate pastor Sue Ellen Westfall, the sister of our current pastor, started a women's circle for mothers of young children, and named it Mary-Martha, a reference to the sisters of Jesus' good friend, Lazarus. As the Bible story goes, Martha was cooking and cleaning while Mary sat at Jesus's feet, hanging on his every word. Martha went to Jesus to complain, pleading with him to require her sister to help her, and he spoke these words: "Martha, you are troubled about many things; only one thing is necessary." What Jesus meant, of course, was that learning about the kingdom of God was more important than a clean house or a hot meal, but we quipped that we were all "Marthas", and that the "one thing" necessary was a casserole.

We became especially close to two of these families and remain so today. Howard and Karen Rivers joined Central in 1988, when their daughter, Charlotte, and Lauren, were infants. A year or so later Peter Schneider and Holly Heuer came to Central with their sons, Tom and David. Peter had moved to Denver to serve as Dean of the College of Architecture at the University of Colorado, and Holly was a Presbyterian minister. Her father and Howard's had been partners in an architecture firm in Monroe, Louisiana, the same town my sister-in-law, Olive, was from, and the Heuers and the Montgomerys had known each other. Our three families bonded, and we mutually endeavored to rear our children in our Christian faith. We engaged in several intentional practices, one of the most meaningful being an Advent study developed by the Presbyterian Church (USA) titled *Whose Birthday Is It, Anyway?*. We met the four Sundays before Christmas for dinner and discussion, encouraging each other to focus on the contemplative aspect of Advent and to resist the commercialism of Christmas. Howard died of cancer in 1999, and Karen and Charlotte later moved to Minnesota to be near extended family, but when we see them on happy—or sad—occasions, it is as though they never left.

Our condominium in Cherry Creek was large enough for the three—and sometimes four— members of our family, but, in order to get to the main level, we had to walk up a full flight of stairs. As Lauren got older, she would stand at the back patio window and look down into the courtyard of the complex, exclaiming, "Look, Mama, neighbors!". But there was no way we could let her go out to play. We began to think about moving.

The elementary school we were assigned to was Steck, located on the other side of Colorado Boulevard from Cedar Court. We took Lauren to visit and to meet the principal, who we all liked. Afterward, we drove around the neighborhood and spotted a "For Sale" sign at 376 Albion Street, just three houses south of the school. We bought the house in May of 1993 and moved in a month later, keeping the condo as a rental, as the real estate market was weak. This turned out to be a godsend when we moved back to our old home during a major new home remodel six months later. I had visions of Lauren rolling out of bed and walking to Steck, but this was not to be. The weak real estate market was symptomatic of other ills in the economy, and schools were cutting their enrichment programs—art, music, and sports. The principal we had all liked was transferred to another school. We contacted St. Anne's Episcopal School, where we had applied a year earlier, and they had a place for Lauren. She started kindergarten there in the fall.

That year Lauren and I began a tradition of taking mother-daughter spring break trips, during which Andy often went fishing in Wyoming or Montana. We enjoyed skiing in Summit County, where my family had a condominium, or in Vail, with friends who had a home there. For several years, we went to Glenwood Springs, where we stayed at the Kaiser House Bed and Breakfast, or the Hot Springs Hotel. One year, when Lauren was in high school, we decided to fly to Cancun. It was there in the Caribbean that she had a nasty encounter with a jellyfish, and we both took our first ride in an ambulance. She recovered quickly and we had a fun time, but from then on Andy invited himself to join us for these vacations, the last of which included road trips to Arizona, and Sandhill Crane-watching in the San Luis Valley of Colorado.

Our family has had its share of disappointments, as all families do, but there were two events I would describe as tragic. The first occurred in 1994. My grandparents were gone by then, and my great-uncle, Elmer, was now the Hester patriarch. Elmer was Granddaddy Hester's younger brother. He had a twin, Elbert, who had died in 1975. When a young man, while visiting my grandparents, Elmer had met my grandmother's niece, Thelma Hagood, also visiting, and they fell in love and married. My grandmother's niece became her sister-in-law, a story I never tired of hearing.

Elmer and Elbert established Hester Hardware and Lumber in 1948. In addition to the normal items found in a hardware store, they carried beautiful housewares, and Thelma helped many Lubbock brides, including me, register their gift selections. Elmer and Thelma were charter members of their church, Westminster Presbyterian, located across the alley from their store. Elbert and his wife, Ethel, were also members, until his death, when she moved to Austin. My grandparents, in whose home a group of sixteen original members met to discuss forming the church, had given the land for its building. The chapel at Westminster is named Hester Chapel.

On February 2, 1994, Elmer picked Thelma up from a visit with her sister, Minnie Mae, and put the car in gear before she had fastened her seat belt. He had a heart attack, and the car crashed into a tree, killing Thelma instantly. Elmer died two hours later in the emergency room. Though he had a history of heart disease, she had no serious health issues, was younger, and might have lived on for many years. Their son, Elbert Thomas (Tom) Hester, whose brother Stewart had died in 1997, suggested to me that his mother's death probably precipitated the death of her sister not long after.

The second tragedy was actually a series of events, set in motion when my cousin, Thomas Wyatt Hester (Tom), Uncle Carl's only son, contracted HIV AIDS and died on July 8, 2002, less than a month after his forty-seventh birthday. Tom had an intellectual disability; from what my grandmother told me, something went wrong at his birth, causing a lack of oxygen to his brain. His mother, Betty Juanita Green, lavished him with love and taught him impeccable manners, and when Carl and his family traveled from Houston to Lubbock to visit all of us, Tom was doted on by my grandparents. (In the Hester family my mother was nicknamed "Betty Ross", and my aunt, "Betty Carl".) Tom attended Texas State Technological Institute, where he studied horticulture. My uncle and aunt had established an elaborate estate plan, including a special needs trust for Tom. Carl had real estate investments, including apartment buildings, which Tom maintained, with his father's help. Betty died of cancer in 1985, and in late 1986, Carl married Elizabeth Schmidt, a talented fashion illustrator and my friend Sherron's "Aunt Lib", which is why the two of us now call ourselves cousins. Carl and Lib had dated in high school, and a series of poems he wrote for her and about her, in a collection titled *Like a Graceful Swan,* indicate she was the love of his life. She was also a devoted stepmother to Tom.

My cousin, Karen, who is a lesbian, maintains our cousin Tom was also gay. Though I respect her opinion, I have my doubts. My parents' theory rings truer for me—that Tom was outgoing and affectionate, and susceptible to those, male or female, who would take advantage of him, either because of his differences, or because of his financial resources. No one knows how he became infected, and it doesn't really matter; we all loved him dearly and grieved his passing. Uncle Carl distributed Tom's estate among his Hester and his Green cousins.

Shortly after Tom's death, Lib was involved in an automobile accident, and then diagnosed with a brain tumor. She died on June 23,

2005, in the nursing home where Carl visited her each day. These multiple losses created a palpable sadness in my uncle's being, leading, I believe, to the events that eventually transpired.

My family traditionally came together around Labor Day for an annual mini reunion near the time of my father's birthday. We celebrated other milestone birthdays together too—Uncle Carl's eightieth with a gathering at Lake LBJ, organized by Tina, and Uncle David's ninetieth with a catered dinner arranged by Karen. But Daddy's birthday on August twenty-third, and at least ten satellite family birthdays around the same time, seemed the perfect occasion for an outdoor gathering at La Colonia, David and Billie's custom home development which backed up to Hillcrest Country Club's golf course and featured eighteen homes built around a large open space. Eventually, the three brothers—Ross, Carl, and David—my mother, and my cousin, Mel, lived within a stone's throw of each other at La Colonia. (I should mention here that my parents were twice married, and twice divorced. They finally settled into a compatible living arrangement with mirror-image homes situated next door to each other, where each could set the thermostat to his or her preferred temperature.)

At these August events, Daddy would cook a huge brisket, and Mother would direct their six grandchildren and David's grandson, Wyatt, in the performance of a skit she had written for the occasion. Uncle David would take the kids out in his golf cart, which is how each of them learned to drive. Uncle Carl would always write a poem—*Ross Roars Up to the Pearly Gates* was an especially memorable one, read by Bo and Tina's husband, Bob, on Daddy's eightieth. Sometimes there was music—a violin duet by Thomas and Neil, or Neil and Wyatt, or a keyboard arrangement by Lili. Joyce Horne Milam (Grandmother's younger brother Boone's daughter) and her husband, Dick, a former Texas A&M football player and West Texas oil man, would always join us, and he would have us in stitches with one of his politically incorrect Cajun jokes. Other surviving cousins in my father's generation—Tom Hester and his wife Consuelo, Beth Hester McCullough (Elbert's younger daughter) and her husband Jim, Kay Hanna, and Don Parr and his wife Judi, would sometimes come. And there were friends who were like family—Dr. Stan Thornton, whose Uncle George, a week older than our Uncle Carl, had been nursed by our grandmother when his own was ill, and Dr. Al Row, Daddy's ophthalmologist, who is married to Olive's sister, Liz. (Olive's sister is Big Liz, and her daughter, my niece, is Baby Liz.) My sister would bring one, or sometimes two of her dogs—whippets and greyhounds—her children. Renée ran Hester Books—the used bookstore my father started after he retired from Caprock—and took it to a new level. She always had an interesting work-related story to share; perhaps the most exciting was the day Larry McMurtry, the best-selling novelist who also owned a used bookstore, stopped in to check out her Texana collection.

So many of my memories center around the Hesters, but I also have fond and funny memories of the Hobbses, my mother's parents—Marion Wilson and Ruth Jewel Sims—and her three brothers and two sisters. Most Friday evenings of my early childhood were spent at my maternal grandparents' home, where we children (Julia and Gerry, mother's youngest siblings, and Randy and I), sat around a huge antique radio listening to *The Shadow*, and *The Lone Ranger*, while Mother cooked with her mother and cared for a younger child or two, and Daddy visited with his father-in-law. Granddaddy Hobbs was a stern but gentle man, an engineer with the highway department for most of his working life. He was deeply interested in the natural world and had built a telescope for viewing the clear Lubbock night sky; in those days we could see the Milky Way any time we liked. His bookshelves were stacked with copies of *National Geographic*, and he had collections of interesting rocks and Indian arrowheads.

These arrowheads had been collected over the years in Yellow House Canyon, the site of an 1877 battle between a combined force of Comanches and Apaches, and a group of American bison hunters. The site was located a few miles north of my grandparents' home, just outside the city limits. As we grew older, Randy and I would often be invited to sleep over after our Friday night dinners. I would share a bed with Julia, who was five years my senior, and Randy shared with Gerry. By then my grandparents had a television, and we would stay up late and watch *The Untouchables*, a series based on federal agent Elliott Ness and his pursuit of the Chicago mob. In the morning, the boys would head out with Granddaddy to look for arrowheads while I paged through movie magazines in my aunt's room, staring at her and willing her to wake up and entertain me. Today, I regret not having gone out with my brother and uncle, and especially my grandfather. It would have been a wonderful opportunity for me to know him better.

Granddaddy Hobbs had built the flat-roofed cinderblock house his family lived in at 3008 First Street in 1947, and painted it pink. It was modest, but there was a beautiful climbing red rose bush outside the kitchen door, which was fertilized regularly with leftover coffee grounds. In summer, Julia and I climbed up onto the roof with our romance novels, slathered ourselves in tanning oil, and soaked up the sun. I hope she gets regular skin exams today, as I do, because we really baked ourselves! The neighborhood was known as Arnett Benson, and included a movie theater of the same name. Julia, Gerry, Randy, and I took in many movies at the Arnett Benson Theatre—horror films like *The Creature from the Black Lagoon*, and epics like *The Ten Commandments*, Disney animated classics, and beach movies featuring former Disney Mouseketeers. Julia outgrew our company along the way, at which point our entertainment expanded to include sneaking out behind her when she left on a date and spying on her and her boyfriends.

Over the years, the Hobbs family grew and disbursed. Uncle Marion, the oldest, who everyone called "Doc", never married, and lived in Farmington, New Mexico. He died in August of 2011. Aunt Mary and Uncle Max were in San Antonio before retiring to Georgetown, Texas. They have both passed on, leaving Melanie (and her children—Sean, Ian, and Kiera), and Mark (who is married to Heika, plus her two children, and their daughter, Ella). Uncle Eldon and his wife, Aunt Mary, had previously moved to Georgetown. They have five children: Mike, Doug, David, Richard, and Denise. I lose track of the number of grandchildren and great-grandchildren, but they are all beautiful; I was with them after Mary passed in February of 2020, just prior to the pandemic lockdown. Aunt Julia and her husband, the Reverend Charles Grisham, live in Temple, Texas. They have two children, Carol and Bryan, who each have children of their own. Julia also has three children (Noelle, Kevin, and Holly) by her first marriage to Leon Cox, and these cousins, too, have children. Uncle Gerry and his wife, Kay, have David, Jennifer, Jerrod, and Amber, and all but David have children. Of my Hobbs grandparents' six children, only Gerry stayed in Lubbock. Mother left and returned.

I retired from my financial planning practice on December 31, 2009, the day I turned sixty. I had guided my clients through the economic crisis of 2008, their (and our) investments were intact and recovering, and our daughter's college graduation was in sight and fully funded. Andy had let most of his employees go during the downturn and had leased vacant space in his office building to architects in need of a cooperative arrangement. In September of 2010, after completing every deferred home maintenance project on my list, reorganizing my filing system, and helping Lauren settle into her own apartment in northwest Denver, Andy and I flew to Honolulu for a three-week home exchange—a time we agree was the most fun and relaxing of our lives.

The one project awaiting conclusion on our return from Hawaii was updating our estate plan, now that Lauren did not need guardianship in the event of our deaths. I remember leaving the attorney's office and getting into the parked car as my phone rang. Time stood still as my brother, Steve, told me he was in Mother's hospital room before handing the phone to her. "Honey, I have a little spot on my lung," she said, "but I feel fine, and I think everything is going to be okay." In fact, my mother, who had smoked cigarettes since her late twenties, had advanced lung cancer. Her doctor told her that with aggressive treatment she might live six months to a year, and without, she would likely die within three to six months. Mercifully, she chose the latter option.

After a couple of trips back and forth from Denver to Lubbock, I decided to stay with Mother until her death. At first, she argued with me about this. "You have a family to take care of," she said, but then admitted she needed a caregiver, and, because I was now retired, I was the obvious choice. A hospice nurse came several times a week to drain a port installed in Mother's back and make certain she was comfortable; her medical care was now palliative.

The four and a half months between my mother's diagnosis and her death was a sweet time, an almost holy time. We brought out old family albums. We played bridge or worked jigsaw puzzles in companionable silence. Mother told me more about her time in Paris where, at age fifty-five, she had gone to live alone in a pension and study French. Aunt Mary came to Lubbock for a week and she and Mother reminisced about their teenage years and remembered their own mother. Marion, Eldon, Julia, and Gerry each came to say goodbye to their sister. Mother told me she had always admired my independence—a reassuring affirmation, as I was sure I had caused her nothing but trouble. Holidays took on an urgent importance—the last Thanksgiving pies I would bake with my mother, our last Christmas with Mother, Mother's eightieth and final birthday celebration, on January 24, 2011. My sister Renée, with whom I had not been close growing up, became a soulmate and a close friend; this closeness has continued, and has been a joy and a comfort.

Daddy shuffled over in his pajamas and bathrobe each morning, carrying a tray with his breakfast—a concoction of three different bran cereals and sliced grapes—a formula for well-being he convinced his brothers to adopt somewhere along the way. Uncle David came around in his golf cart each morning to deliver the papers, still in *his* pajamas. His wife, Billie, who we always referred to as "the boss of our family", had died in 2005, and after a period of mourning, he invited five single women to his house for dinner, at the same time. Marcy Bateman, the widow of a brilliant Tech law professor, wound up being the one who chose to marry him. Uncle Carl now lived between Lubbock and Bayside, Texas, and his house was directly across the open space from Mother's, so she and I could watch him through her picture window, walking toward us, tall and erect, wearing a weathered, short brim Stetson. One day Mother asked me wistfully, "Who's going to take care of these old men when I'm gone?"

Mother died peacefully, early in the morning, on March 24, 2011. I was with her, and Jeff, who now lived in Pagosa Springs, Colorado, was in the next room. He sat with Mother while I first went next door to get Daddy, then called our three Lubbock siblings, the pastor, the hospice nurse, Carl and David, Gerry, and the Texas Tech Health Sciences Center, to whom Mother had donated her body for medical research. The Reverend Davis Price had come to Covenant Presbyterian Church thirty years earlier. Though Mother had not attended worship for years, she adored Davis, and he had visited her regularly during her illness. He was like a member of our family, a big handsome man who had played football at Austin College before attending Princeton Seminary and marrying his high school sweetheart, Janet. It was Janet who gave Daddy "permission" to wear Bermuda shorts and his Austin College "Fear the Roo" t-shirt to church the previous summer. "God doesn't care what you wear," she assured him, though, I am embarrassed to admit, I did.

Once we were gathered, Davis led us in a short, bedside service. Then the five children and Daddy regrouped at his place, to share memories of Mother with Davis, who would officiate at a memorial service at the church ten days later. In the 1980s, psychological research revealed that children growing up in the same family each experience that family in a unique way, as though it is a different family—a micro-environment—for each child. Multiple factors contribute, but each child has a unique personality and his or her parents respond to that in an appropriate (or sometimes, inappropriate) way. And of course, parents are going through things in their own lives at different developmental stages in their children's lives. So it is not surprising I learned things I had never known about my mother from my siblings that morning. Randy told a particularly poignant story about a friend his age who lived on our block. The boy's father was verbally and probably physically abusive to him and his mother, and he struggled in school. Mother took it upon herself to schedule a conference with his teachers to share his difficulties and ask for their compassion. It is hard to believe there was not more anyone could do, but this was in the 1950's, and abusive parents and spouses still went unchecked.

Back in Denver, I cast about for my next act. I took over the billing for Kenney Architects and helped Andy market for new clients. I taught insurance in the CFP certification program at Metropolitan State University. I would often ask my students to give short reports on their organization, to help the others understand different product distribution systems. In the fall of 2012, I had several TIAA representatives in my class. They were an impressive group, smart and personable, and one day as I sat at the reception desk in Andy's office, with time on my hands, I went to their company website. The company had three regional offices: Charlotte, Dallas, and Denver. All were hiring and, on a lark, I uploaded my resume. I received a call almost immediately and was recruited to join the next class of trainees, which would begin in January of 2013.

The class was large—fifty or so individuals—only four of us women. Most of the men were closer to Lauren's age than mine, and I wondered if my purpose in being there was to identify a future husband for my daughter, so I always invited her to join us when we met for "happy hours" after work. My computer skills, which had become stagnant, were refreshed. One spring morning, I was crossing the street from my bus stop to my thirty-six-story office building at the southeast corner of Seventeenth and Broadway (directly across the street from what had been the Great-West Life towers, where I had worked twenty years earlier), and recognized Roger Ferguson—president and CEO of TIAA at that time and headquartered in Charlotte— walking alongside me. Mr. Ferguson had been vice-chairman of the Federal Reserve and would later (it was rumored) be on President Biden's short list for Secretary of the Treasury. I introduced myself and he and I had a nice visit as we entered the building and rode the elevator up, letting him off on the executive floor. Roger, as he insisted I call him, assured me I had a great future with the company.

So when I received a text a few weeks later from my good friend, Holly Heuer, telling me about an opening at the Presbyterian Foundation, I told her I was not looking for a job. "Sherry", she drawled, "just promise me you'll look at the job description." I gave her my word, and she sent me a link.

Do you remember the scene in the Mary Poppins movie, when Jane and Michael Banks write a job description for their ideal nanny? Mr. Banks reads it, tears it up, and throws it to the wind. It reconstitutes itself and floats into Mary Poppin's hands. She lands with her

open umbrella at the front of the line of nannies waiting to be interviewed at the Banks home, and asserts she is the perfect candidate
for the position. That positivity reflects the way I felt after reading the
job description on the Presbyterian Foundation website for Ministry
Relations Officer. I knew they were looking for me and felt bad for
keeping them waiting.

I updated my resume to highlight my volunteer development
experience with several non-profits (Families First, Girls Scouts, St.
Anne's Episcopal School, and Rocky Mountain Children's Choir) as
well as my involvement at my own church as chairperson for the stew-
ardship and endowment committees. In my cover letter, I referenced
my experience, two years earlier, as my mother's caregiver, and the
importance she shared with me of leaving a legacy. I uploaded these
items and waited for a response. Following multiple phone interviews
and a trip to Louisville, Kentucky, my date of hire was July 8, 2013.

Working for the Foundation was my dream job, so rewarding I
hesitate even now to call it work. The culturally diverse region I covered included Texas, Oklahoma, Arkansas, Louisiana, Colorado, and
a little slice of Nebraska. I organized my wardrobe into "uniforms"—
heels and a chalk-striped sheath for Dallas and western boots and
dressy jeans for Scottsbluff. The higher the temperature outside in
Houston or New Orleans, the lower the thermostat was set inside the
church. A jacket or sweater was a must, and I still had to explain, on
occasion, that my teeth were chattering not because I was nervous, but
because I was not accustomed to this much air conditioning. My good
friend, Sarah Krause, gave me a carry-on Tumi bag she had retired
upon her own retirement from Northern Trust, and I became so proficient at packing it that I could get ready to leave town in twenty minutes. A line in my job description had read "must be able to lift travel
items overhead". Whenever a man, or sometimes a younger woman,

jumped up to help me with my bag, I insisted "Thank you, but this is part of my job description."

The MRO position, which utilized some of my best gifts—meeting people, making presentations, and crunching numbers—in essence involved bringing the resources of the Foundation to individual Presbyterians, churches, and mid-governing bodies—presbyteries and synods. We sought to invest funds, but also to help grow generosity among church members and help structure legacy gifts to their church and other Presbyterian entities, such as seminaries, schools, children's homes, and camp and conference centers.

My colleagues were an outstanding group of men and women with whom I became close during my seven and a half years with the Foundation. A third were pastors; the others had varied and interesting backgrounds, and we shared a desire to serve Jesus Christ, and a love for his church. The Vice-President we reported to was Stephen Keizer, a tall, handsome man not much older than my son, who had three sons of his own, all outstanding athletes. He was devoted to his family and to us, and to helping each of us succeed. He supported my desire to participate in the Certificate in Ministry program at Austin Presbyterian Theological Seminary, and on its completion, presented me with my framed diploma when my peers were gathered at one of our quarterly meetings. These meetings, held around the country in our different regions, were so much fun I still smile when I remember them.

Ten months after I joined the Foundation, Andy had a stroke. At first, he thought he was having a migraine, but an MRI revealed otherwise. His doctor at the time seemed more concerned about not getting sued for not immediately sending Andy to the ER than he did about helping with his recovery. I made an appointment with Dr. Elizabeth Bloomfield, my internist, who was, thankfully, accepting new patients. Within twenty-four hours of meeting Andy, Liz had contacted each of his doctors for his records and designed a course of medication to prevent a reoccurrence, which she continued to monitor and adjust on a weekly basis. In addition to his vision being affected, he had a constant headache and wanted to sleep most of the time. His perception of time was affected, and he often missed one of the frequent doctor appointments on his schedule, as well as other meetings, sometimes with clients.

There is never a good time to have a stroke. But Andy's occurred on May 19, 2014, four months short of his sixtieth birthday. The disability policy I had sold him, which he had continued to increase as his earnings grew, paid benefits in the event of an illness that occurred before his sixtieth birthday, or in the event of an accident that occurred before sixty-five, should he not be able to perform the duties of an owner-architect. Though he tried to work, both his attorney and his doctor recommended he not, and after a year, he sold his firm to another architect and his office building to another business owner, at a time when the market had rebounded for both. Financially, he was whole. My job at the Foundation provided excellent health insurance benefits, so he received the best care possible and, for all appearances, has fully recovered.

I have always enjoyed golf, so twelve years ago when Betsy Mangone asked me casually (as I was leaving an event at the Denver Foundation) if I played, and invited me to join a group of women scheduled to tee off at one of the many Denver area municipal courses, I accepted with pleasure. The Golf Stars, as we now call ourselves, play monthly from March to October, and this has become one of my most important friendship groups. It was originally organized by Betsy and Ellen Fisher, a disciplined writer and my impetus for this book. I have never known a group of sixteen more accomplished women, many of them with backgrounds in development, and their shared experiences were beneficial to me in my years with the Foundation.

My Monterey High School friends constitute another such group. Linda, Jessica, Lindi, Meredith, Jane, Mary Lane, Teri, Marge, Sherron, and Kay—and of course Phyllis—are all women I try to stay in close touch with, because they have each touched my life. The Birthday Group, and my St. Anne's Moms group, I write about elsewhere. It has been said that friendship is the spice of life; I say it is the salt—an essential ingredient for good mental, and even physical, health. There was a time when I had a therapist on call if I had a problem to work through, but in recent years I have learned that a walk with a good friend—Sarah, Jan, Anne, or Leslie to name a few—serves the same purpose for free, with the added benefit of exercise.

I return now to the story of Uncle Carl. After his second wife, Lib, died in 2006, Carl was advised to begin distributing his assets to avoid estate taxes, and he made generous gifts to me and my siblings and cousins each Christmas. He updated his will to make us and our fathers his heirs. He provided my brother, Steve, who he named executor, with a copy signed on October 3, 2007, and showed him the file cabinet where he kept the original. This was bittersweet. As grateful as we were for Carl's generosity, we knew that what he had accumulated should be going to his own son. We tried to fill the void left by Tom, and then Lib, with visits, calls, cards, and letters. My cousin, Tina, and Lib's niece, Sherron, were especially devoted. It was Tina who published the poems he had written to Lib, and in the foreword, he describes my cousin as "Boss Lady in Training", a title he bestowed on her after her mother died.

Shortly after Mother's death, Carl began to show up at family gatherings with a woman named Billie, not to be confused with David's first wife, our dear bossy aunt and Tina, Karen, and Mel's mother. Billie was eight years younger than Carl. Carl's health was declining—he had survived prostate cancer, as had his two brothers—and now his big, generous heart was giving him problems. He was totally deaf and showed signs of dementia, wandering off and being returned home by the police on more than one occasion. On the one hand, it was a comfort to know our aging uncle had female companionship, but on the other was a nagging feeling of discomfort. David and Daddy wanted Carl to move to Carillon, the Lubbock retirement community my father now lived in, and David took him there for a tour and an assessment. In hindsight, that probably triggered what happened next.

Early the morning of June 23, 2015, Carl and Billie left Lubbock without saying goodbye to either of his brothers. They drove an hour and a half to the Howard County courthouse in Big Spring. They applied for a marriage license and convinced the clerk to waive the three-day requirement between its issuance and the performance of a ceremony by the Justice of the Peace. The next day our uncle did not remember he had remarried.

I do not doubt Billie loved Carl; there was nothing not to love about our uncle except perhaps his stubbornness, a decidedly Hester trait that contributed to Andy's and Olive's decision years ago to form a "Spouses of Hesters Support Group", open to anyone married to someone with Hester blood in their veins. Four months after the marriage, Carl bought Billie a house she had long wanted in Bayside. When they returned to Lubbock for the ninetieth birthday party we planned for Carl at Hillcrest Country Club, she was overheard talking to his investment advisor about changing beneficiaries on his retirement accounts.

Although she was cordial to Andy and me when we visited in Bayside for a weekend, and later to me when I visited Carl in a nursing home in Refugio, Billie discouraged visits from Tina. Once she went so far as to instruct the staff at the nursing home he stayed in while Billie attended her granddaughter's wedding not to allow Tina into his room. The seventeen months between Carl's third marriage and his death on November 25, 2016, at age ninety-one, were marked by a series of falls and stays in nursing homes. My brothers and Tina had urged him for years to sign medical powers of attorney so we could assure he received proper medical care, but he consistently refused. Instead, Billie became his *de facto* POA. I do not believe he was well served by his decision.

Twelve days after Carl died, Mel, Uncle David's stepson, suffered a fatal heart attack. A joint memorial service was held for the two of them at Covenant Presbyterian Church in Lubbock. Billie did not attend, but held a second service for Carl on January 7, 2017, in Woodsboro, Texas, which members of her family, and ours, attended. We were friendly to her three adult children, but it was clear they were as suspicious of us as we were of their mother.

On March 31, 2017, David's second wife, Marcy, died, and again our family gathered for a memorial. Marcy, who had three grown sons of her own, had been a good wife and companion to David. Though she was wealthy in her own right, she was frugal, an avid gardener, and a teacher of English as a second language to adult students. Whereas our Aunt Billie had been a Red Raiders fan, Marcy enjoyed taking David to performances of the Lubbock Symphony Orchestra. She was known for the delicious fruit salads she brought to family events, but otherwise, she was not a very good cook, and Daddy looked for excuses to avoid accepting her dinner invitations. David, however, was loyal, and when Daddy once commented in private that Marcy's steamed rice was crispy, David responded, "Well, maybe Marcy likes it that way."

By the time of Marcy's death, we were engaged in a legal dispute over Carl's will. The original will he had written in 2007 had disappeared from the file cabinet. When Steve submitted a copy of the signed original for probate at the Rufugio County Courthouse, Billie—who had hired one of the top estate attorneys in Corpus Christi—contested it. Tina's husband, Bob Garrett, is the capital bureau chief in Austin for the *Dallas Morning News*, and one of his many contacts recommended another top attorney in Corpus to represent us.

My uncle was frugal and may not have wanted to spend the money to update his will after re-marrying, although his dementia was more likely the cause of this neglect. Regardless, at one point I calculated there were eight attorneys, including a judge and a court-appointed executor, involved in settling his estate. Eventually, after being significantly reduced by legal fees, it was divided roughly into two shares, one going to the ten heirs (nine, after Mel's death) on our side of his family, and one going to Billie. None of us felt entitled to Carl's assets and would have been happy to have them go to one of the churches or charities he so generously supported. But we do not believe what happened, neither the legal battle nor the final division of his estate, is what he would have wanted. Billie has now passed on as well.

Uncle David died in 2018, shortly after his ninetieth birthday, at Carillon, where he had moved after Marcy died. Daddy, who lived on the same floor, visited him daily, pushing a walker and bringing a gently read copy of the Lubbock *Avalanche-Journal*. David's body had grown weak, but his mind was still sharp. Karen, his younger daughter, who had sold her share in a co-housing project in Oakland and now spent her time between Pahua, Hawaii, and Grand Lake, Colorado, came to Lubbock to stay with him until his death. Wyatt, his only grandchild, was finishing a degree in accounting at Tech and preparing to sit for the Chartered Financial Analyst exam. He and my sister played hearts regularly with David. He was also attended to by Kelley Bui, an engineering student at Tech. David and Billie had sponsored her Vietnamese family's migration to the United States years earlier — the Buis were one of several such families they sponsored. David was beloved by all of us, and by many others, including a family friend named Brian McPeak, who he considered an adopted son.

My father, the oldest of Wyatt and Nettie Hester's three sons, pressed on. His knees creaked audibly when he got into or out of his reading chair, where he spent most of his time with Callie, one of his two cats, in his lap. Tammy, his other cat, was usually on his bed. Whenever I called Daddy, the exchange went like this: "Ross Hester here." "Daddy, it's Sherry, how are you?" "Not bad for an old man. How are things in Denver?"

He started planning the celebration he would have on his one hundredth birthday shortly after he turned ninety—a "family reunion", as he described it, at Steve and Olive's, "because they have such a lovely house for entertaining." He would say to me, "I hope you'll be able to make it," and I would tease him by saying, "I don't know, I might need to organize some drawers that day, or clean out my purse." He would laugh; then I reassured him that I, and my whole family, would be there, and that I would bake a pineapple upside-down cake. It was his favorite, and he told me his mother always made one for him on his birthday when he was growing up.

By the time the World Health Organization declared COVID-19 a pandemic in March of 2020, assisted living and nursing homes in the United States had begun taking measures to keep their residents safe, and Carillon was no exception. Though Daddy was still living independently, he was confined to his room, and his meals delivered to his door. His dementia was worsening, and we knew there were days he ignored the food he was brought and ate Snickers bars instead, accompanied by the Franzia *Crisp White* boxed wine he favored. He did not really understand what was going on, but understood it was affecting people all over the world. When weather permitted, one of my three Lubbock siblings met Daddy outside for a visit.

Jeff offered to move Daddy to Pagosa Springs, Colorado to wait out the pandemic with him and Jan. My youngest brother and his wife, Jan Carolyn VanWagenen, had met in high school, in Austin, where Mother had moved when she and Daddy divorced the first time. The two married shortly after their graduation. Jan's parents had both died when she was young, and she had been reared by her maternal grandmother, and then, together with her two brothers, by her father's stepbrother and his wife. Daddy often told me that Jan was the only one of his daughters-in-law who called him "Dad". Except for their first house, which they rented, Jeff and Jan have designed and built every house they have lived in, each to perfection, especially the one in Pagosa, where they moved in 2004. But this beautiful home is on multiple levels, and the older siblings felt it best for Daddy to stay at Carillon.

Jeff got special permission to come into Daddy's apartment and take his cats for relocation, as there was no one to clean the litter box. We put Daddy's name on the waiting list for an assisted living apartment, and one became available that fall. On September 26, 2020, Steve, Renée, and I entered Carillon wearing full personal protective equipment, and winnowed our father's now meager possessions down yet again, to what would fit into a one-bedroom efficiency. As always, he was cheerfully resigned.

When a vaccine became available a year after the pandemic began, we thought we were home free. Our visits with Daddy resumed, and he continued to plan his big birthday party. But before he received a booster shot, after the Delta variant reared its ugly head, my father went out to dinner with Randy and Renée on a Friday night in July and he contracted Covid. Andy and I were sitting at the Bull and Bush in Denver on July 28, 2021, with two friends from the Presbyterian Foundation—my hand-picked successor, the Reverend Joseph Moore, and Brad Masters, Vice-President of New Covenant Trust Company— when I received a text conveying this news. Disturbing as it was, I had faith my father would recover.

Over the next week, I continued to check in with my Lubbock siblings and with Daddy, who was now isolated in the nursing home unit at Carillon. When I called him the afternoon of August fourth, he sounded confused, and kept talking about his hip replacement. I reminded him the surgery had taken place years ago, but he carried on about it until I suggested he eat his dinner and said I would call him back. I called the desk nurse, who told me Daddy had gotten out of bed to visit the restroom and had fallen. He had broken the femur of the leg of his hip replacement and the Carillon staff was now waiting to hear back from his primary care physician about scheduling a surgery. Daddy's orthopedic surgeon was on vacation, but a young doctor—a classmate of Steve's son, Thomas—was called on to perform the needed surgery on August sixth. The operation was successful but very hard on my father, and conversations with my siblings and the nurses' station gave varying reports on his status from one hour to the next.

Andy had gone to Old Baldy in Wyoming for his annual book club outing on August tenth, and I was sitting on Jan Netting's patio having a cocktail and telling her what had transpired in the past two weeks. When she offered me a second drink, I declined, telling her I needed a clear head, as I suddenly realized I needed to get to my father. Minutes later, I walked through my back door, sat down at the kitchen table, and booked a Southwest flight to Lubbock, through Dallas, leaving at seven o'clock the next morning. My sister picked me up at the airport and drove me to University Hospital, the teaching hospital for the Texas Tech Health Sciences Center.

We donned full PPE and entered Daddy's room. He recognized us immediately. His condition had stabilized and Covid beds were needed, so the hospital was readying our father to return to the nursing home unit at Carillon. I said, "Daddy, I love you. I'll be waiting for you at Carillon when you arrive." He said, "I love you too, Sherry."

That was my last exchange with my father, who was not conscious of our presence when the ambulance delivered him. Steve and I stayed on, and my brother Jeff arrived from Pagosa Springs, but Daddy never regained consciousness, though his body labored on throughout the night and through the following day, during which I sat by his side. Renée and I were with our father when he died, peacefully, the evening of August 12, 2021, just eleven days short of his ninety-seventh birthday.

The service for Daddy, held at Covenant Presbyterian Church, with its new pastor officiating, was restrained, due to Covid concerns. But it was meaningful, with each of Daddy's three grandsons participating. Neil sang *On Eagles' Wings* in his beautiful baritone voice, and Bo and Thomas eulogized their grandfather, both holding back tears. Lauren left Stella with Alex to drive from Denver with us, and Liz flew in from Mexico. Only Lili, who was halfway around the world in Lithuania, was absent. The youngest of Daddy's four great-grandchildren, little Cece, still nursing, was in her mother's arms. Friends and family, former Caprock employees, and members of the congregation were masked and in attendance. After the service, we returned to Steve and Olive's house, where their First Methodist Church friends had set up a lovely lunch. Playing with Thomas and Callie's children, and holding the baby, helped to replace our feelings of loss with those of wonder and expectation.

My friend Denise Sanderson brought me a beautiful book, *The Orphaned Adult*, after Daddy died. The cover description reads "understanding and coping with grief and change after the death of our parents". I realize how fortunate I was to grow up knowing all four of my grandparents, and to have my parents in my life for so long. My mother lives on for me in her granddaughters—Lauren, Liz, and Lili, three remarkable young women, two of whom are named after their grandmother. And my father lives on in his grandsons, of whom he was so proud.

Lauren Elizabeth Kenney Berv, Stella's mother, I have written of extensively. She and her father are my cheerleaders for this memoir.

Clara Elizabeth (Liz) Hester, born September 7, 1989, to Steve and Olive, is fluent in Spanish, and traveled throughout South and Central America on her own before settling first in Oaxaca, then Mexico City. She is an artist and a designer who, when in school, excelled in academics, acting, and athletics. She is tall and elegant, the niece I always imagine—like those in Victorian novels—will be my travel companion in old age.

Lilien Aurora Hester (Lili), born April 18, 1991, to Jeff and Jan, was named Bonnie Rose by her parents. She was a phenomenon, who at age three could identify and describe every dinosaur known to walk the earth. While still a teen she changed her name, and today is an exotic persona who loves music, and cats. She speaks fluent Russian and lives in Vilnius, Lithuania, where she is a translator for *Bored Panda* and an activist for LGBTQ rights.

Boyd Wyatt Fisher, my son, I have written extensively of in another section of this book.

Thomas Langford Hester, born April 5, 1984, is my godson, an Eagle Scout and an oil company executive. As he grew up, his parents, Steve and Olive, reminded him often that he was a Hester, and to conduct himself accordingly, just as my grandparents had reminded their three sons years earlier, according to Grandmother's memoir. Thomas is married to Callie Ann Baker, an attorney and Instagram aficionado, beautiful inside and out and the mother of their three children, Stella's second cousins—Thomas Langford, Jr. (Langford, born June 21, 2017), Elizabeth Beilman (Birdie, born October 22, 2018), and Cece Ann, born September 8, 2020. Thomas is a devoted father, a kind and gentle man like his own father, my brother.

Dr. Neil Randal Hester, born August 17, 1990, to Randy and Lyn, is an academic, a gifted musician, and an athlete—an all-around great guy who has always been modest about his many achievements. After attending Texas Tech, where he sang in the men's chorus, he received his master's degree and his PhD from the University of North Carolina at Chapel Hill. After teaching at McGill University in Montreal, he is now researcher/professor of social and personality psychology at the University of Waterloo, near Toronto.

On a recent visit to my Lubbock siblings, I was reminded by one of my brothers of something our father often said, that "any story worth telling is worth embellishing." Daddy's cousin, Tom, emailed me recently, when I asked for confirmation of a story I had grown up hearing, "As a volunteer for our public library history desk, I have come to distrust family accounts."

However, I want Stella to know that I have tried not to embellish, and that what I have recorded here—though perhaps not totally accurate—is all true.

Photos

*With Hester grandparents (foreground)
and great-aunts Eula, May,
and Sybil Horne*

David, Carl, and Ross Hester

My Hobbs Grandparents

*Mother at the
Lubbock Little Theater*

David and Billie

My siblings and my Hester cousins

Carl and Lib, Tom inset

Andy and I on our wedding day

With Mother and Daddy

*Gerry, Julia, Eldon, Mary, Betty,
and Marion Hobbs*

Andy and I, Bo and Jean, and Lauren

Randy, Lyn, and Neil

Renee with Brooks, Rosie, and Tyler

*Steve and Olive, Thomas and
Callie, and Liz*

Jeff, Jan, and Lili

*Hester cousins Tina and Karen,
Tina's husband, Bob Garrett*

Andrew Martin Kenney

Papa

ANDY KENNEY GREW UP in Denver at the corner of Franklin Street and Louisiana Avenue, across the street from South High School, where his mother, Laurene Gardner Willson (Laurie) graduated in 1942, and where he graduated thirty years later, in 1972. His father, Robert Edwin Kenney, built the family home in the early fifties. It was a three-bedroom brick ranch which fronted Washington Park, and through the years Laurie and Bob, and then Laurie alone, rearranged the floor plan to meet their needs at the time.

Bob had been an outstanding athlete at Regis High School, where he lettered in basketball, and then at the Colorado School of Mines. Laurie was a popular beauty. Their romance was in full bloom when he enlisted in the Army in April of 1943, and during his basic training Laurie traveled by train to visit him, chaperoned by Bob's mother, Ruth McFarland Kenney (Ruthie), and her mother, Grandmother Mack. Bob served on both the European and the Pacific fronts during World War II and saw unspeakable death and devastation. Like most men of his generation, he declined to discuss his experiences, and like many, he attempted to forget them through the numbing use of alcohol—in his case, bourbon. To this day Andy hates the smell of it.

Even as his social drinking deteriorated into dependence, Bob was never abusive—but could sometimes be embarrassing, once falling asleep during church, and refusing to be awakened, so that the children finally walked home without him. He became sober after an intervention by friends and family, but then suffered from multiple cancers, and died too young because of them. Laurie loved her husband deeply, and remained devoted to keeping his memory alive, wearing his sweaters, and sharing memories of happy times they enjoyed living in the basement of his parents' home during the housing shortage after the war. There, after marrying on May 14, 1946, they welcomed first a son, Stephen Robert, born August 23, 1947, and then twin daughters, Anita Diane (called Diane from birth) and Suzanne Marie, born June 25, 1949, into their lives. Andrew Martin, born September 21, 1954, after they had moved to the new house, was the bonus baby Laurie conceived after miscarrying her fourth child.

Andy was a "good" child, obedient and respectful. He perceived his mother's challenges and committed not to aggravate them. He tagged along with his older siblings to the park across the street, where they spent hours each day with other neighborhood kids until Bob whistled for them to come home for dinner. Before he started school, he and his mother rode the bus all over Denver (Laurie never learned to drive), seeing Doris Day movies and creating memories, and an intimacy they enjoyed to the end of her life.

Bob was raised Catholic—Laurie, Episcopalian. She planned to convert when they became engaged but changed her mind at the last minute. She agreed, however, that the children could be reared in Bob's faith tradition. While she worshipped at St. Michael and All Angels on Sunday morning, they attended mass down the street with Bob at St. Vincent de Paul. A pivotal incident occurred at St. Vincent when Andy was in the fourth grade, at his church-sponsored school. Sister Mary Oscar, an elderly nun, asserted to the class that anyone who was not Catholic could hope to go no further on the path to Heaven than Limbo, a decidedly Catholic concept. Andy could not buy the argument that his saint of a mother could not go to heaven while his hard drinking father and grandfather could, just by virtue of their being Catholic. He argued with his teacher, who charged down the aisle toward him, arm raised, the substantial cross around her neck swinging. Andy covered his head to protect himself, and when she struck him, she fell to the floor, hurting her wrist and demanding one of Andy's female classmates summon the principal. Andy spent the next few hours locked in a dark closet until his older brother came for him on his bicycle. "You're in big trouble," Steve warned him; but in fact, Andy was a hero to his family for standing up for his mother.

Andy was a "lapsed Catholic" when I met him in 1984, and he struggled with his faith. After all, he reasoned, what good had his fervent boyhood prayers done to cure his father of the diseases of alcoholism, and then cancer. I invited him to attend church with me at Central Presbyterian, where the Reverend John Wilcox assured him it was right to question dogma, and even all right to question God, concepts foreign to the Catholic church under Pope John Paul II. Andy and I took a year-long Bible study course together titled *Kerygma*, which at its root means "proclamation". At the conclusion of the course each participant wrote his own brief statement of faith. Andy's begins, "I believe that I am a part in an unknowable context, over which is a governance that is good and God."

Though Bob attended "Mines" before he enlisted, when he returned, he enrolled at the University of Denver under the GI Bill. He was gregarious and charming, and was drawn to a career in hospitality, a course of study DU has long been known for. But the draw of the family business was stronger. His father, James (called Jim), had founded Kenney Construction, which built many of Colorado's high-ways, dams, and bridges, and his older brother, Jim, Jr. was already active there. Bob left college before graduating to join them.

Laurie grew up at 246 South Sherman Street with her mother, Stella Bertha ("bright star") Steuland Willson—*Gommy* to her grandchil-dren—her sister, Julie, and her brother, Murt. Laurie's father, Murton Sr., called *Poppy*, suffered from mental illness, probably bi-polar dis-ease, and lived in the attic of the house. He was a brilliant illustrator; in Andy's words, "he designed things that got built." Andy grew up surrounded by his grandfather's framed illustrations. Laurie inherited his artistic ability, which she shared through her homemade birthday cards and beautifully painted Easter eggs. Julie married early and had a son, Jimmy. She and her first husband divorced, and she married Jack Kennedy, with whom she had Johnny.

Murt left Denver to study architecture and design at Harvard, and later studied in London as a Fulbright scholar. He married Margaret, who everyone called Margi, and settled in California to practice. They had a daughter, Sydney, and sons Geoff and Ned. Sydney, a talented musician with children of her own, died recently after a long battle with cancer. Andy and his siblings were especially fond of her.

Gommy loved botanicals and could name any plant. After being widowed, she worked as house mother for a DU sorority. Sometimes Andy stayed with her there to be doted on both by his grandmother and by the college girls. At the end of her life, *Gommy* moved in with Bob and Laurie. Andy remembers his grandmother's hospital bed set up in his room during his first year of high school, during which time he slept on the living room floor.

Though Andy never really knew his maternal grandfather, his father's father was larger than life. Papa called everyone, including Andy, "Murphy". One day he pulled up in front of the house on Louisiana in his pick-up truck and found Andy playing by himself outside. "Hop in, Murphy", he said, "we're going to buy you some tennis shoes." Andy, five or six at the time, was thrilled about the shopping trip, and assumed it had been cleared with his mother. When he was dropped off an hour and a half later, wearing a new pair of Keds, his mother was fuming. She warned Bob that his father had better not ever "kidnap" one of her children again.

Jim Sr. (and later Bob) were active in leadership within their trade associations. Once, when he was attending a national convention in New Orleans, he walked into Antoine's, the famous French Quarter restaurant, with a group of engineers, and without a reservation. When the maître de greeted them, family lore has it, he said, "Murphy, give us the best table you have." The man, whose name turned out to be Murphy, and who perhaps thought he had forgotten an important patron, did just that.

The office of Kenney Construction was in northwest Denver; the construction yard was in Commerce City. Jim Sr. and his two sons traveled back and forth between the two. Bob got to know Denver's famous Italian restaurants, Gaetano's, Patsy's, and Pagliacci's—all located near the office—and Laurie would sometimes ask him to bring homemade Bucatini pasta and meat sauce home for dinner. Of course, waiting for the food involved sitting at the bar, and Bob became friends with several local Italians and fellow Catholics. One, a high school acquaintance named Roxie, was invited to be Andy's godfather. Andy was with his father twenty years later at Roxie's funeral, attended by olive-complexioned men in dark suits, shirts, and ties, looking for all the world like they had stepped off the movie set of *The Godfather*. When Andy was introduced as Roxie's godson, they all bowed low and said with the deepest respect, "Roxie was your godfather? Oh, I'm so sorry, I'm so, so sorry." Andy is great with accents, and when he tells this story, it really comes alive.

Andy's older brother, his male Kenney cousins, and eventually Andy worked summers at the construction yard. The weather was hot, and the work was hard. It was also dangerous. Jim Sr. died as the result of a tragic accident in June of 1963, when the boom of a mobile crane collapsed, crushing the cab he was operating it from. Bob, always close to his father, was grief-stricken. Ruthie lived for a time with Bob and Laurie, and then with Jim, Jr. and his wife Mary Lou, in whose home she died on March 29, 1976.

There are not many pictures of Andy as a child, which is typical for the youngest. The few I *have* seen portray him as tow-headed, small, and somber. But he has described many happy childhood experiences to me. On Sunday afternoons after church, the extended family often gathered at the home of Ruthie and Papa at the southeast corner of Sixth Avenue and High Street. Andy's siblings and cousins—James III (Jimmy), David, Peter, Mark, Mary Michael (Michael), Daniel, and Mary Allison (Allison)—hung out on a screened-in porch with a huge collection of comic books Ruthie had purchased at the corner drug store, Joy Pharmacy, where she also took them on occasion to sit at the soda fountain and order lime and cherry phosphates. Andy's favorite comic characters, besides the classics—The Three Musketeers, Robin Hood, Prince Valiant, etc.—were Donald Duck and his nephews, Huey, Dewey and Louie, and the chipmunks, Chip and Dale. He specifically detested Archie.

Once a year Ruthie and her sister, Virginia Louise McFarland Smiley, would have a "girls' getaway" to Las Vegas, and would bring silver dollars home to Ruthie's grandchildren. Andy treasured those silver dollars, but they, along with his stamp collection, were stolen by an intruder who broke into and ransacked his family's home when he was a teen. Often, in the summer, Aunt Louise would pick Laurie and her children up and take them to Valley Country Club, where Bob was a member. Sometimes, while Louise supervised the pool activities,

Laurie and Bob would golf, an activity they enjoyed together throughout their married life, often in resorts they visited through Ports of Call, a popular Denver-based travel club.

Andy went from elementary school at St. Vincent, where the children were required to be uniformed and polite, to Byers Junior High, where a contingent of the boys crafted weapons during shop class, to South High. On most days during his three years at South, he rolled out of bed, delivered the *Rocky Mountain News* to the homes on his route, made it to school by the time the first bell rang, then delivered the evening *Denver Post*. He enjoyed high school and had friends in multiple groups. He was too small for most sports (until as a rising senior he grew almost seven inches in one summer!), but he enjoyed tennis, encouraged by his friend, Dave Weidner. The Weidners, who pushed their son to excel in every area, were somewhat responsible for Andy attending the University of Colorado, or for that matter, any college at all.

Having grown up around the construction business, Andy was interested in engineering and architecture. But though he was always placed in honors English classes, he struggled with math, and wonders today if the multiple head injuries he sustained as a child could be responsible. His high school counselor, Sally Peres, suggested he consider trade school. He was offended, but to give Ms. Peres the benefit of the doubt, Andy was very good at mechanical drawing, like his mother's father, and perhaps she saw him as a future draftsman. Bob was ill and Laurie was too occupied trying to hold the family finances together to provide Andy the guidance he needed. So, he just did what Dave Weidner did. When Dave took the SAT, so did Andy. When Dave applied to CU, Andy did too, and in the fall of 1972, he entered the four-year Environmental Design program in Boulder, where he and Dave shared a dorm room, and, eventually, an apartment.

Andy thrived in college, both socially and academically. The course of study he chose was rigorous, but he found time for work and play. His part-time jobs included working the night shift at a nursing home (which allowed him time to study), being a security guard, driving a delivery truck for Frito-Lay, and lifeguarding at Boulder Reservoir. His senior year he lived in Vail with a girlfriend from St. Louis, where he stocked shelves for City Market and spent time on the slopes. Somehow, he managed to commute to Boulder for classes and studio time, and he graduated with the attention of his dean, Dwayne Nuzum, who invited Andy to work for him after graduation, and in whose name Andy has established a permanent endowment fund for architecture students at the University of Colorado Foundation.

Andy's work for the Boulder firm Community Services Collaborative, where Nuzum partnered with landscape architect and planner John Feinberg, involved traveling around the state, assisting small towns like Central City, Brush, and Alma in obtaining community development block grants from the Department of Housing and Urban Development, and then administering the grants. One of his more interesting projects involved working with the Central City Opera to upgrade properties they owned in the historic mining town (before gambling became legal there and in neighboring Black Hawk). While exploring the crawl space beneath a house built not long after Colorado became a state, in a crouched position, Andy lost his balance and fell backwards, thrusting his hand and arm through something that felt like a drum. His flashlight revealed the skeleton of a dead mountain lion which had no doubt sought shelter and become trapped years earlier.

It was in the context of this work that Andy met—and subsequently married—his first wife, Nicky, a bond underwriter and partner in the firm Newman and Associates, where I worked with multiple clients, one of whom referred me to Andy a few years later for financial services. By then, Andy had entered graduate school at the University of Colorado in Denver, working toward a master's degree in architecture, and the circuit riding life was not conducive to study or marriage. A good friend and fellow architecture student, Jerry Gloss, had worked for Nowak, Stevens and Associates in Denver since 1978, and he introduced Andy, who was also hired. Andy worked for the firm until graduating, and even stayed on for a short time after becoming licensed, before starting his own firm, Kenney Architects, P.C. in 1983.

Throughout my years with Andy, I heard many people ask what kind of work he specialized in, commercial or residential. He always answered that he designed many houses, but that most of his billings were commercial—a statement, I think, about where the money is in architecture. After we were both divorced but before I agreed to marry him, Andy warned me that architects do not make much money. There are stories, and at least one movie, about prominent architects who died penniless, and numerous, less dramatic examples of architects who wanted work in their portfolios so badly they allowed their fees to be whittled away until a project was no longer profitable. Andy did not fall for that strategy. He was an excellent businessman, striving to do good work for a diverse group of clients, delivering a quality product at a fair price. He had no delusions of grandeur, and did not seek the limelight, but rather strove to provide a good income for his family and his employees. He stood behind the work his staff performed and tried to provide the training and resources they required. If they were unhappy, he encouraged them to find another opportunity.

Andy always wanted a partner, and tread lightly into several relationships, but they never worked out. In 2010, he hired Jennifer McDaniel, a young woman who was reared in Chicago and educated at the University of Texas College of Architecture in Austin. Jennifer had both the talent and the temperament Andy desired. Jen stated she needed flexibility. She had a baby boy who sometimes accompanied her to work and played quietly under her desk. At other times she worked from home. Andy was apprehensive at first, but was soon convinced he got more than he paid for with Jennifer. Though their partnership was never official, she was as committed as any partner could be, and he referred to her as such.

After his stroke in 2014, Andy looked for a buyer for Kenney Architects. Jen knew a young architect, Rob Forslund, who was interested. Andy hoped Rob and Jen would become partners, but that did not materialize. Today Rob owns Chord Design Studio, formerly Kenney Architects, and Jen owns Fluency Architecture & Design. On occasion, Andy now does contract work for Jen, and he still refers to her as his partner. We both think of her as another daughter, and love her and her husband, Loren, and their children, Evan and Sophie, as members of our family. Andy was honored to attend Sophie's adoption ceremony as a special friend. The whole family joins us regularly for our Kenney Christmas-Eve-Eve party.

I am always amazed at the number of projects Andy completed during his career. No matter where we are in the metro Denver area, he will point to a medical office building or a branch bank and say, "I designed that", or to a multi-story office tower and say, "I did work in that building." Among his most fun projects were the design of Izakaya Den on South Pearl Street, and a custom home for our dear friends Don and Wendy Milliman near Denver's Polo Club North neighborhood. Among his most prestigious projects were the interior design of the corporate offices and dining facilities in the Great-West Life Towers at Interstate 25 and Orchard Road, historic preservation of the Colorado Trust lobby at 1600 Sherman Street, and a stunning pool house at a Fisher & Fisher-designed home in the Denver Country Club neighborhood. That project, introduced to him by his friend and mentor John Prosser, earned his firm the cover of the May 2015 issue of *Colorado Homes & Lifestyles*. The vision statement on his full-color brochure, *Shaping the future and preserving the past*, truly described the breadth of his talent and ability. He was licensed to practice architecture in six states and completed projects in England and Ireland as well.

As important as Andy's career was to him, his family came first. He was a devoted father who had no fear of changing diapers or being the parent in charge of a crying or croupy baby. He drove morning carpool more often than I did, and regularly attended the soccer, softball, volleyball, tennis, and swim events Lauren participated in. He offered to help—sometimes a little too much, in my opinion—with her school projects. He cleared his calendar for PTA meetings. He presented Lauren at Le Bal de Ballet, a debutante presentation of the Denver Ballet Guild, where he was required to dance, which he does not enjoy. And when he walked Lauren down the aisle at Central Presbyterian Church on June 18, 2017, to become Alex's bride, and toasted their marriage at the Grant-Humphreys Mansion, his love for her was transparent.

Andy always knew he wanted to be a father. He adored his two nieces, Kathleen Marie, born July 26, 1975, and Kristine Ann, born October 17, 1977, to Steve and his wife Maryann. The girls traditionally spent Christmas Eve with their grandparents, Bob (Papa) and Laurie, while their parents sang in the midnight service at Most Precious Blood Catholic Church. Andy, home from college for Christmas, delighted in the girls in their matching holiday pajamas. As Kathy's godfather, Andy attended her first communion. Two years later, I attended Kris's first communion with him, a new experience for me—children of seven or eight years old, girls dressed in white, celebrating the Eucharist for the first time. Kathy married her CU sweetheart, Ted Zeiger, and converted to Judaism. They are parents to Eliana and Mateo, Stella's second cousins, and, fortunately for us, live in Denver. Ellie had her Bat Mitzvah at Temple Sinai on July 16, 2022, where she read from the Torah, and presented her D'Var Torah (a word of Torah, or speech) on the rights of women to bodily autonomy. Kris married Joe Sams, whom she met while attending Eckerd College in St. Petersburg, Florida. They live in Page, Arizona, with their son, Cooper, and thrive on the natural beauty of the Grand Canyon. Their wedding took place there, on the shores of the Colorado River, where Kris steered us by boat to a sandy beach, wearing her full-length wedding gown.

Andy's sisters, Diane and Suzanne, just six months older than I, were dressed in matching outfits as children, as was the custom with twins growing up in the fifties. I cannot tell them apart in photographs, though Andy can, and they had some fun "trading places" in school and with their friends. Today they are very different but remain close to each other. Diane is married to John Sulsona, born in New York City to Puerto Rican parents. He is father to John and Rene, who each have children and grandchildren (and Rene, a great-grandchild) of their own. Diane has the pleasure of being a great-great-grandmother without ever having had to endure childbirth herself. Suzy had meaningful relationships with other women earlier in her life, but today seems content with the constant company of her cat, Mortimer. She had wanted to study veterinary medicine, but in the late sixties and early seventies this was still a totally male-dominated field, a regret she feels to this day. Diane made us all proud when she returned to Regis University to earn a degree in business at the age of forty.

Steve's profession was geology; according to Andy he could identify any rock or formation presented to him. We have a few beautiful samples from his extensive collection on display in our living room, and Stella is enthralled with them. Maryann is a retired physical therapist. Though Andy's mother was a wonderful hostess who enjoyed entertaining, she did not care much for cooking. Laurie often said the gift she gave her daughters-in-law was that we would never have to hear our husbands say, about the food we prepared, "That's not the way my mother did it."

When Stella was born in June of 2020, during the COVID-19 pandemic, the Kenney family had to be satisfied with pictures of their new niece and cousin, although Kris paid her a masked visit. But in December of 2021 we held our traditional Kenney Christmas Eve Eve party, and Stella met Andy's family for the first time. She was mesmerized by them, and charmed them to pieces with her big blue eyes. Steve and Maryann gave her a cloth doll, and she scooted up and down the basement stairs in her fancy silk dress, in pursuit of Ellie and Mateo, holding the new doll close. Recently I observed to Lauren that Ellie is now old enough to babysit Stella, as Kathy and Kris did her, and we are looking forward to some quality Kenney cousin time.

Andy has often lamented the fact that there is no history of longevity among the men in his family. But he is determined to challenge that trend, and we both look forward to celebrating the future milestones in our granddaughter's life.

Photos

Andy's mother, Laurene

Andy's father, Bob

Laurene's mother, Gommy

Laurene's father, Poppy

Laurie and her siblings - Julie and Murt

*Bob's father, James Sr. (Papa) w/
Suzy, Diane, Andy, and Steve*

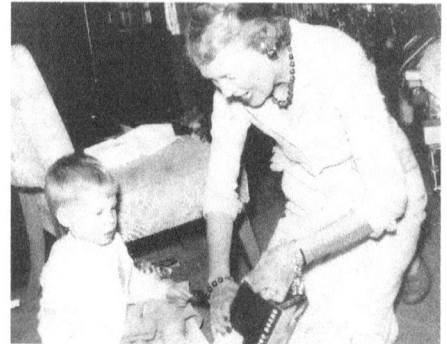

*Andy with his Kenney grandmother,
Ruthie*

Bob and Laurene

*Bob's brother, James Jr. (Uncle Jim) and
wife Mary Lou Bastien*

*Steve and Maryann, Kathy
and Kris*

Diane and John Sulsona

Suzy and Laurie

Andy and his sweetheart

Andy and his angels—Jennifer, Kathy, and Lauren

Kris Sams-Kenney, Joe, and Cooper in Arizona

The Zeigers, at Eliana's Bat Mitzvah

Boyd Wyatt Fisher

Uncle Bo

BOYD WYATT FISHER WAS born November 23, 1967, on Thanksgiving Day. His father, William Douglas (Bill) Fisher, had deep brown eyes and dark hair. I had hazel eyes, and light brown hair. It was a surprise to us both that our baby had blue eyes and red hair, and the milkman jokes circulated in my hospital room. My grandfather, Wyatt Langford Hester, gray-haired for as long as I could remember, informed us all that when he was growing up his friends had called him "Red". Bo's middle name comes from Granddaddy, and my mother's next younger brother is Eldon Boyd Hobbs. But to be honest, Bill loved football, and wanted to name his son—called Bo from birth—after Boyd Dowler of the Green Bay Packers.

Just as they had always adored me, their first grandchild, Wyatt and Nettie adored Bo, their first great-grandchild, and as far as they were concerned whatever he did was precocious. Grandmother kept a notebook with a page for each letter of the alphabet, and for a while tried to record every word Bo spoke for the first time. She gave this up as his vocabulary exploded.

Bo was the first grandchild in both our families, and Cliff Fisher, "Popo", who was a prominent dentist in Lubbock, was especially smitten. He and Nana Ann would walk over to our small, rented duplex every evening to peek at the baby, just about the time I had rocked him to sleep and lain him in his crib. Their stealthy steps on the nursery's hardwood floor invariably woke Bo, to my chagrin and their delight. Now that I am a grandparent myself, I totally understand.

When Bo was a baby, I walked him daily in a wicker perambulator I had purchased at a "junktique" store. As he grew older, I took him often to Wagner Park, where he loved to swing and to run around the playground. The park, located in Tech Terrace, was catty-corner to a fabric store, and I stopped in often to buy material for the cute jumpers I made for Bo on my Singer. On Sunday mornings I dressed him up and took him to John Knox Presbyterian Church, where my family and I were charter members. Granddaddy Hester could not wait to get to the nursery after worship to pick up his great-grandson and show him off during the fellowship time.

Mr. Rogers' Neighborhood, first broadcast on February 19, 1968, and *Sesame Street*, first broadcast on November 10, 1969, were morning staples at our house, great entertainment for a toddler. But in the evening, we watched the grim nightly news, Walter Cronkite reporting increasing numbers of American troops being deployed to Viet Nam, casualties rising, and the country deeply divided over its involvement in an unpopular war. Thankfully, Bill was excused from the draft due to his family status.

On May 11, 1970, Bill and I arranged for a babysitter and went to a drive-in movie. A non-family sitter was an anomaly because we had great-grandparents, grandparents, uncles, and aunts always eager to keep Bo. But this was a Monday—a work, and school night. By the time we got to our destination on the north side of town, it was raining. We sat in the car listening to the radio, with the announcer warning of severe weather, as the sky blackened. We headed back home, but by then the rain was a deluge, and the streets were flooding. That was about the time the first of two tornadoes hit Lubbock. Frantic about our son's safety we drove south on Avenue T in fear our car would stall, and we would be stranded. When we reached Broadway, we saw that the front windows of Margaret's, the retail women's apparel shop I had worked at a year earlier, had been blown out, and two women huddled inside. We stopped to invite them into our car and again headed for home. When we got there the duplex was empty; the Fishers had left a note saying they had picked Bo and the sitter up and were going to their church, Forrest Heights Methodist, just a few blocks away. We and our two new friends joined them, where we spent the night—together with many others—huddled on the floor of the church basement with a few blankets, feeling lucky to be alive. The tornadoes, among the worst ever to hit the area, destroyed over a thousand homes and apartments and ten thousand vehicles. They killed twenty-six people and injured over five hundred. The twenty-story Great Plains Life Building (now named the Metro Tower), Lubbock's tallest building, was declared condemned by the Amarillo company that insured it. Cliff Fisher's dental office was on the sixteenth floor of this building. Dr. James Granberry, an orthodontist and a good friend of the Fishers, had been elected mayor of Lubbock just nineteen days earlier. Jim told Cliff the building was structurally sound, and that it was safe to go into it, even though it had no power. As a result of that counsel, Cliff, Bill, and I spent the next two days climbing up and down sixteen rubble-strewn flights of stairs—with flashlights—rescuing boxes of patients' dental records, including, incidentally, a plaster mold of Buddy Holly's teeth.

Later that same year, Bill and I divorced. Bo and I lived briefly in a rented apartment near the campus of Texas Tech, where I was a student, before moving to Austin, where I continued my education at the University of Texas. We lived in a subsidized government housing project, but it was clean and new, and even had a pool. The Austin scene was compelling—Viet Nam war protests on the campus encircled by live music and bottomless pitchers of beer. Sometimes it was a challenge for me to stay focused on my studies and my part-time jobs—assisting a professor in the College of Business Administration and Management, and grading essays for the head of the philosophy department.

My next-door neighbor was also a divorcee, and her two sons, Kelly and Trey, became Bo's best friends. They were supportive when, at age five, he decided to give up his pacifier, after years of cajoling and pleading on my part. They went with him to bury it in the woods behind our apartment and had a little ceremony. That night Bo cried himself to sleep—inconsolable—but woke up the next morning his normal exuberant self, never looking back. Bo was also friends with Ellen and Nick, children of a couple of professors for whom I babysat. These four children all came to his fifth birthday party.

I was married again in the fall of 1971 to Tom Caldwell, a law student at UT who had also grown up in Lubbock and graduated from Monterey High and Texas Tech. Tom loved Bo and had a no-nonsense step-parenting style. His older sister, Ann, who was married and lived in Dallas, had a son, Clay Trantham, about the same age as Bo. The two boys enjoyed playing with each other when we got together in Austin, Dallas, or Lubbock. Ralph and Gene, Tom's parents, were older than mine, and were very kind to Bo.

On one of the regular trips Tom and I took to Lubbock to visit our parents, Bo spent time with my Hester grandparents at their house. When I went to pick him up Granddaddy took me aside and shared with me that he had discovered Bo and one of the neighbor boys exploring the upstairs attic—an old-fashioned dormer style space, steeply sloped, with exposed insulation—holding lighted candles. I could see in his eyes the terror he felt as he imagined two little boys and three elderly residents dying in a wood-frame house fire. My theology acknowledges God as Creator, involved in a deeply personal and loving way with creation, but not as a puppet-master interfering with natural laws. Still, that day, I felt God's hand on all our lives, and felt in my heart God had a special purpose for Bo.

During my time in Austin, Bill Fisher graduated from Texas Tech and began studies at South Texas College of Law in Houston. I sometimes drove Bo to Houston to visit his father, who at other times drove to Austin. We remained on friendly terms. During his three years in law school, Bill met and married fellow student Mary Ann Denning, a warm and gracious woman. She and Bill had one child, Katharine, Bo's sister, now married with two children, Wyatt, and Rosie. Yes, my beloved grandfather's name, shared by many Hester male progeny, jumped family lines. Bill and Mary Ann eventually moved from Houston to Fort Worth, and then divorced, but Bo remains close to them both. Bill has married again, and Mary Ann is in a long-term relationship.

In December of 1972, I received a Bachelor of Arts degree in sociology, then took a full-time job in the UT law library. I loved the work and decided to take the LSAT, then applied for entrance to the University of Texas School of Law in the fall. I was accepted, but in May of 1973 Tom received his LL.M. and accepted an appointment as briefing attorney for the Court of Civil Appeals in San Antonio. We moved in June, after Tom passed the bar exam, to our new home, a three-bedroom brick house with a big front porch located in an old, established neighborhood—just east of Brackenridge Park and across the parking lot from Earl Able's, a restaurant famous for its fried chicken. I went to work for Fidelity Union Life Insurance Company. Mary and Max Allen, my mother's sister and her husband, lived in Windcrest, just a few miles north of us. On the weekends Tom sailed with Max on Canyon Lake, I visited with Mary, and Bo played with my cousins, Melanie and Mark, who were just a little older than he. Mark loved to tease Bo, once convincing him to eat a chili pepper too hot for human consumption. When they see each other now, at Hobbs family gatherings, they fall back into their easy companionship.

We spent two years in San Antonio, during which time Bo attended The New Age School—located within walking distance of our home—where he made friends easily. He still remembers his teachers: "The Fox" was librarian, Shea taught art, Barry taught science, and Terry taught math. Bo learned to read quickly, motivated by his love of the super-hero comic books used as primers at New Age.

In August of 1975, we and our dog, Germaine, moved to Castle Rock, Colorado. Tom began his new job at Haskins & Sells in downtown Denver, I reported to the local Fidelity Union office in University Hills, and Bo attended second grade at Castle Rock Elementary, until I became discouraged for multiple reasons and moved from Colorado back to Texas, this time to Arlington, where I worked for Fidelity Union in its home office in downtown Dallas. That spring Bo's teacher wrote me to say she was scheduling parent conferences, but that Bo was doing so well and was such a star student there was no need for me to come in. In the summer of 1976, I moved back to an apartment in southwest Denver with Tom, and Bo went to live with Bill and Mary Ann in Houston. I felt this was best for Bo; I was unsure about my marriage to Tom and wanted stability for my son. But it was a difficult adjustment for us both, and each of us harbors sadness, even today, about our separation.

In May of 1977, Bo and I accompanied my parents and my brother Steve to my sister Renée's graduation from Davidson College, an outstanding Presbyterian school located outside Charlotte, North Carolina. After the baccalaureate and graduation ceremonies, in which my sister was awarded a degree in economics, we toured Biltmore, in

Ashville, then drove to Atlanta to help my sister settle into her first apartment. She was to begin work at Trust Company Bank, a position her friend and mentor, Davidson alum Harlee Branch, Jr., a prominent attorney and business executive, had helped her secure. On the long drive home, Bo talked on my brother's CB radio. This was a popular thing to do in the seventies, made so by the Country and Western song, *Convoy*, by C.W. McCall. Bo's "handle" was Big Red. One of the long-haul truckers he conversed with, as we traveled across the miles, said, "Red, you're funny, and you're smart. I hope someday you decide to run for president." This was—and is— the effect of Bo's engaging personality on people.

Later that same summer, after Bo flew back to Houston to begin fourth grade, I received a phone call from Harold Kountze, a vice-president at Colorado National Bank, which his family had founded. Mr. Kountze had sat next to Bo on the plane and was calling to tell me how much he enjoyed the flight, and how impressed he was with Bo's intelligence and good manners. I give the credit to Mary Ann.

In the fall of 1977 Tom and I purchased a home at 3140 South University Boulevard. Bo made good friends the following summer thanks to a lost cat. After our previous cat, Vincent—named for my favorite poet Edna St. Vincent Millay—was run over in our apartment parking lot, I adopted Buck and Clyde, feline brothers sired by different fathers, we surmised, as they were litter mates who bore no resemblance to each other. When Clyde went missing in our Southern Hills neighborhood I walked door-to-door looking for him, carrying flyers with a drawing by my friend and work colleague Min King, an artist from Boston and Kennebunkport.

When I rang the doorbell at 3152 South Josephine Street, an attractive woman answered it, as two cute kids peeked out from behind her. They were Bobbie Anton and her children, John, and Cindy. I introduced myself, explained my reason for being there, and showed the three of them the sketch of Clyde, for whom they promised to be on the lookout. I then commented that John and Cindy appeared to be about the same age as my ten-year-old son, who was arriving in a week for the summer. Bobbie, who became a dear friend and remains so today, said, "Well, just send him over—the kids play kick-the-can in the street all day." When Bo got to Denver, he went around the block, where, sure enough, there was a gang of kids: John and Cindy, Scott Evans, David Scofield and his siblings, and Carol Goudy, now Bollman. He was instantly accepted into the group. Scott was recently lost to a tragic death, but John, Cindy, and Carol remain friends.

Bo attended Bellaire High School, at that time one of the highest ranked public schools in the country. He was active in student affairs—receiving recognition from Houston mayor Kathy Whitmire, and being selected as one of six Texas seniors to receive the International Youth Year Award presented by the U.S. Secretary of Education. Still, he had his insecurities, as most teens do, and he went through a rebellious phase, exacerbated I'm sure by my second divorce, initiated in the summer between his sophomore and junior years. When he arrived in Denver in the summer of 1985, he had shaved his head, had a collection of tee-shirts with off-color or anarchist messages, and wore an ear cuff for extra shock value (not so shocking by today's standards). He hung out at Wax Trax, just down the street from the Washington Irving, where I lived, and played punk rock at a volume not suitable for apartment living. The summer culminated in his totaling my car.

I married Andy in December of 1985, and Bo graduated from Bellaire in May of 1986. We attended his graduation, along with my parents and siblings, who came from Lubbock and Austin, and my Uncle Carl and his son, Tom, who lived in Houston. In June, Andy and I treated Bo to a trip to New York City, where we had lunch at Tavern on the Green and dinners at Windows on the World and Harry Cipriani, after which we attended the Broadway musical, *Cats*. Bo showed his disdain for us by sitting down to wait outside of Tiffany's while we browsed inside, and by walking almost a block behind us most of the time. I was terrified of losing my son in NYC, long before the day of mobile phones. Still, when we returned to Denver, I surprised my professional colleagues by hiring Bo to answer the phone, assist me with filing, process the mail, schedule appointments, and run errands. At my insistence he wore a white shirt and khaki pants to the office. Bo was one of the best assistants I ever had.

Bo was a National Merit semi-finalist, and had planned to attend the University of Texas at Austin in the fall of 1986. In the spring of his senior year, however, he changed his mind, deciding to remain in Houston with his girlfriend, who was two grades behind him. Not long before graduation he interviewed with an admissions officer at the University of Houston who offered him a full academic scholarship. He majored in anthropology, and after a junior semester abroad in London, with a side trip to Israel and Egypt, was back in Denver for a time. Lauren was almost two, and Bo suggested we all dress for afternoon tea, a British tradition he had come to enjoy. I love tea parties, and prepared both sweet and savory treats. My twenty-one-year-old son told me, tactfully, that the cucumber slices on my finger sandwiches were too thick.

While in Denver Bo purchased a motorcycle, a Honda 650 CC. It was hard for me to argue convincingly against it—Tom had owned a BSA 650 in Austin that we had a blast riding throughout the surrounding Hill Country, and my father had picked my mother up for their first date on a motorcycle—but I knew how dangerous it was. The only thing I could do was to pay for the best helmet available. Bo had fun riding out Highway 285 and into the hills with his friend Mike Franzmann, who also owned a bike, but I told him that if he planned to stay in Denver, he needed to find a job. He left our condominium early one morning shortly thereafter to report for day labor, but had a dangerous fall on Cherry Creek Drive North, which was icy from the sprinklers at Pulaski Park, just a few blocks from where we lived. A homeless man helped him to right his bike and get out of the traffic, but he decided at that point to leave Denver, which he did in late May. He returned to Houston by way of Lubbock, where he stayed with his Granddaddy Ross, and Ringgold, where he visited his Nana Ann's brother, Coy Fite, and Dallas, where he reconnected with friends he had met in London. He then headed southwest for the annual Kerrville Folk Festival. He remembers the exact date—June 4, 1989—because he awoke to the news of the Tiananmen Square Massacre. From there he returned to Houston to look for part-time work and complete his final year of college. Riding was not much fun in Houston, a city known for its freeways and traffic congestion, and Bo soon sold his motorcycle.

Almost two years after Tom and I became members of Central Presbyterian Church, eleven-year-old Bo attended two weeks of Vacation Bible School in June. Stan Love, whose son, Tom, was Bo's age, taught the boys' class, and I assisted. In August, Bo and Tom Love attended a week of church camp together at Black Forest Camp & Conference Center outside Colorado Springs. When we picked Bo up, he was tired and dirty, but immediately asked if he could be baptized, which he had not been as an infant. He would only be in Colorado another three days before returning to Houston for sixth grade, but when I called our associate pastor, Gary Ziegler, and asked if he could arrange the baptism, he did.

Nine years later Bo had a more powerful conversion, in Houston, when a kind and humble Black man named Jerome witnessed to him outside of an Eckerd drug store, after Bo had spent the night drinking with friends in a bar and before he was to host a keg party that afternoon. In a letter dated August 13, 2003, on its fifteenth anniversary,

Bo describes this transformational experience in detail, and reaffirms his faith in Jesus Christ.

The next day Bo attended a Black "Full Gospel" church, then settled into a Baptist church that nurtured his faith. Just over a year later he met Chris Simpson, pastor of New Wine Christian Fellowship. He became so active in this small, non-denominational church that I became concerned it was a cult and flew to Houston to investigate. After attending New Wine's charismatic services, a different worship style than I was accustomed to, I decided it was just that—different— and that if it was meaningful for Bo, I would support it.

At New Wine, Bo became friends with Jean Haney, whose family was from Lufkin, in East Texas. Jean attended a conference in Denver in the summer of 1994 during a time Bo was staying with us, and she visited in our home, now in Hilltop. Jean had beautiful blue eyes and thick, wavy black hair, and an easy-going temperament that provided good balance to Bo's sometimes intense nature. We liked Jean immediately, and it was clear Bo liked her too. A year later, the two of them traveled from Houston to Lubbock for a visit with the Hesters and the Fishers. My father gave Bo two twenty-dollar bills and advised him, "You'd better take this girl to dinner and ask her to marry you—it's not going to get any better than this."

Bo and Jean were married by Chris, their New Wine pastor, at Trinity Episcopal Church in Houston on September 28, 1996, in a beautiful, traditional wedding. Lauren, who had just turned nine, and Jean's niece, Anna, were flower girls. Our Denver friends, Kent and Glenda Winker, who had been best man and matron of honor in our wedding, attended, as did Bo's friend Carol Bollman, along with all my family from Lubbock, and Austin. Uncle Carl and his second wife, Lib, and his son, Tom, held a big barbeque at their small nearby ranch the day before the wedding, and the kids—Lauren and her cousins, Thomas, Liz, Neil, and Lili—went on a hayride and fed the cattle. Bill and Mary Ann Fisher, and Andy and I, co-hosted the rehearsal dinner. I was so happy for my son I barely slept the night before the wedding. Bo and Jean are perfect for each other; they recently celebrated their twenty-fifth anniversary.

In 2008, doctors diagnosed Chris Simpson with cancer, and he died a year later. At his request, Bo served as interim pastor of New Wine—which had moved from Houston to Pasadena in 1996—and then as its permanent pastor, a ministry he shares today with Jean. Bo and Jean are very involved in their greater community, where he helped organize an ecumenical group of pastors who meet regularly to pray for its citizens. Bo is on a first name basis with the mayor, and is known by many community leaders.

Bo and Jean do not have children of their own but have been wonderful friends and mentors to the children and youth in their lives. They are especially delighted by and devoted to their nieces and nephews. They have given me some sweet "grandkitties". Percy, Monie, and Jessie are now in cat heaven, but Caesar, though quite old, hangs on for the tilapia dinner Bo prepares for him each day. Oliver and Oreo, who showed up more recently in the church parking lot, were immediately adopted into the family, providing endless hours of entertainment, and—being cats—only conditional love.

Photos

Bo and his parents

Bo in grade school

On the subway in NYC

Bo w/ Lauren and me, dressed for tea

*Bo's wedding day, w/ Nana Betty and
Granddaddy Ross*

*Jean, w/ bridesmaids Anna
and Lauren*

Just Married!

*Bo and Jean, w/ grandkitties Percy,
Monie, Jessie, and Caesar*

Bo - walking his talk

Lauren Elizabeth Kenney Berv

Mama

LAUREN WAS BORN AUGUST 20, 1987, at Swedish Hospital in Denver, and named after her grandmothers, Laurene and Elizabeth. She was baptized by the Reverend John Wilcox, at Central Presbyterian Church, on October 18, 1987, with grandparents, aunts and uncles, and cousins in attendance. She was a beautiful baby, and Andy and I loved putting her into the stroller on Saturday mornings and showing her off at *Printemps*, the luxury French department store that had a brief presence in the Denver Design Center. I always dressed her in pink, as she had very little hair, but I still found myself explaining after many a compliment that she was a girl baby. When she finally did grow hair, it was fine, and full of static electricity. She complained of her hair being "ecstatic" and refused to let me style it. We had our share of mother-daughter hair wars.

Lauren was a sensitive child with a contrarian streak, an introvert, content to entertain herself and energize alone. Putting her in time out was like putting Brer Rabbit in the briar patch—she liked nothing more than sitting in a corner with a book, which earned her the nickname "busy bookworm". Reading was truly her first love and writing her second; her former bedroom and our basement are filled with boxes of her journals.

Because I worked full time, Lauren had a caregiver, Elisa Vela, who had recently married and come to the United States from Ecuador. From the time Lauren was six weeks old, until she turned fifteen months, Elisa came to us daily. She adored Lauren, cooing and singing and speaking to her in both English and Spanish. Sadly, for us, Elisa and her husband, Henry, moved to Connecticut with his parents, to work for a wealthy family whose matriarch had created the Gund bear. When they returned to Denver a few years later and began their own family—two beautiful daughters, Samantha, and Amanda—we reunited, and have remained friends since. Bob Kenney, Andy's dad, died at about the same time Elisa left, so it was a difficult period for us, though Lauren was too young to understand the double loss. After spending days with our good friend, Karen Rivers, for three months, and then with another short-term caregiver, Lauren entered the Montessori School in Greenwood Village, where she thrived and set out on a path of excellence in education that would truly define her as a life-long learner.

Lauren loved learning—in the Bible Story Room at Central, at Montessori and St. Anne's Episcopal School, and at the various summer camps she attended at the Denver Museum of Nature and Science, where she was once thrilled to dissect a lamb's brain. After I first took her to St. Anne's for observation and acceptance into the next kindergarten class, we were told she seemed more reserved than the other would-be kindergartners, and were asked to reapply the following year, which we did. This meant she entered kindergarten having just turned six, and able to read and write. That year she wrote and published an article in the St. Anne's newsletter entitled *How I Met Mother Irene*, her account of meeting the Episcopal sister who founded St. Anne's. Mother Irene had read *The Tale of Peter Rabbit* to

Lauren's class on the one-hundredth birthday of its publication, and then invited Lauren to read to her. Then, together, Lauren and Mother Irene made carrot salad for the class.

In the spring of 2002, when Lauren received a call from Susan Reid, head of the middle school at St. Anne's, who asked, "Do you know why I'm calling?" our daughter replied, "Am I in trouble?" Mrs. Reid informed her she was class valedictorian and would need to prepare a speech to present to her class. Lauren was thrilled, and a little surprised. She had not taken this honor for granted, as she and Martin Erzinger, who was named salutatorian, had enjoyed a friendly competition since kindergarten. She suggested to Martin they prepare a dialogue, which they delivered to their classmates at the graduation ceremony. The elegant ivory dress Lauren designed and wore still hangs in the closet, waiting for Stella to discover it. After the ceremonial speeches, and prior to the awarding of certificates, each eighth-grader was lauded by one of his or her teachers. Brenda Stockdale, who spoke about Lauren, described her thus: "We will remember Lauren for her compassion, her independence, and her self-professed absentmindedness." She nailed it.

When Lauren was six years old and in first grade, a friend in the neighborhood got a new puppy, a cockapoo. Lauren fell in love with it and asked for a dog. We told her dogs cost fifty dollars and she would need to save the money, thinking that would be the end of the discussion or, at least, buy us a little time. Her allowance was only a dollar a week, paid out in dimes designated for sharing, saving, and spending. We underestimated her resolve and her desire, however, and it was no time before she had the money. Except for the dime that went into the offering plate each Sunday, the entire allowance was saved, for weeks. Gifts from grandparents went unspent. And to put her over the goal, Lauren sold rocks, door-to-door, to the neighbors. We contacted the breeder in Fort Morgan, and learned there were no cockapoos available, but a yorkie-poo could be had for a hundred and fifty dollars, three times what Lauren had raised, and a bargain. We drove on a Saturday to pick up the prize—a tiny ball of fur Lauren named Inky, so black we could barely see her eyes. We brought her home and loved her dearly until she died in the fall of Lauren's junior year of high school.

There was another pet, a fancy mouse named Polo. Lauren originally bought this mouse as a surprise birthday present for her friend, Shannon—with the consent of Shannon's mother, of course—but between the time of the shopping trip to PetSmart, and the day of the party, Lauren bonded with Polo and could not part with him, so another mouse was purchased. Andy and I had tickets to a Broncos game scheduled at the same time the girls were to be picked up for the party in a limo, so I asked another mom, Anne Sneed, if Lauren could come to her house with the gift mouse and wait with her daughter, Mary, for their ride. Anne agreed, after I promised her Lauren would never give Mary a mouse.

We did have another mouse event, however, when Lauren was in seventh grade, after Polo had to be euthanized due to a case of ulcerative dermatitis. We had engaged Greg St. John, a math tutor who came highly recommended, when Lauren entered seventh grade and John Dicker's math class. The first day of school, Mr. Dicker had declared that no one made an "A" in his class, and Lauren was determined to prove him wrong, which of course she did. Another of Greg's students had a fancy mouse with babies to give away, and Lauren wanted two females. We owned all manner of mouse accessories at this point, including a two-level cage with wheels and toys, so we agreed, against our better judgement. Within weeks we had a litter, a cage full of tiny pink creatures that looked like pencil erasers. Inky went wild. We could only conclude our adult mice were not both female, and leaned on Greg for his adoption services, which he felt guilted into providing.

We were soon back to one mouse, who died eventually; but, for years thereafter, the lingering scent of cedar shavings, which had lined the mouse cage, remained in the basement, where the mice had lived.

Greg became a regular addition at the gatherings we held with our special St. Anne's friends, whose kids he also tutored. This close-knit group began with three families, the Curtisses, the Kellys and the Kenneys, whose daughters, Caroline, Anne, and Lauren entered kindergarten together. We carpooled with these families, and the girls played soccer on the same team. Halfway through first grade, the moms—Vicki, Deb, and I—started a girl scout troop for which sixteen girls signed up. Emily Leuthke came to St. Anne's as a fourth grader, and her mother, Paula Armstrong, soon became a good friend and, as a nurse practitioner, our troop medic. Girl Scout Troop 1196 had lots of fun together doing crafts, singing songs, planning camping trips, and conducting public service projects. One favorite outreach activity was baking dog biscuits to take to the Dumb Friends League. Whenever a special flag ceremony was scheduled, there was a rush to attach the badges our daughters had earned to their vests and sashes, sometimes using the more conventional needle and thread, but often resorting to glue guns and staples. At the end of sixth grade, with six girls remaining—our four, Kristen Hagebak, and Jessie Larson—our troop disbanded. We used a portion of our funds for a mother-daughter dinner before turning the balance in to the Council.

One of Lauren's most admirable qualities is her loyalty. I was the undeserving beneficiary of it her third-grade year when I volunteered to provide caramel apples for her class party at Halloween. Another mom, the same one who had sent the limo around for her daughter's birthday party, volunteered to help, and suggested we buy the apples at Rocky Mountain Chocolate Factory. "No, no," I insisted, "they're easy to make." The result was that half the apples were professionally made—beautifully decorated with sprinkles, wrapped in cellophane, and tied with black and orange ribbons. The other half were stuck together in a pool of caramel that had slid off the waxy apples and onto my paper-covered tray during the ride to school. It was a humiliating moment, but Lauren valiantly insisted "I want one of my mommy's apples."

On April 20, 1999, in the spring of her fifth-grade year, two students at Columbine High School, located just fifteen miles from our home, engaged in a shooting spree and attempted bombing that left twelve of their classmates and one teacher dead. Lauren's class listened to the horrific event play out in real time on the radio; her teacher, Mrs. Fleming, had a daughter at the school. Andy and I hardly knew how to process this tragedy—known today simply as "Columbine"—ourselves, much less how to interpret it for our child. We felt woefully unprepared and relied heavily on our pastors, Mark Ramsey, and Amy Miracle, and on the school, whose head was Ramsay Stabler, for guidance and support.

Two and a half years later, on September 11, 2001, terrorists flew planes full of passengers into the twin towers of the World Trade Center, effectively setting off the United States' declaration of a war on terror and resulting in troops being sent to Afghanistan and, later, Iraq. Ironically, we had enjoyed a recent vacation on Long Island in August of 2001—four days at a friend's cottage in Southampton and another four at Sunset Beach on Shelter Island. As we flew above New York on our return to Denver, we looked down on the Twin Towers. I promised Lauren, who had just turned fourteen years old, that when she graduated from high school, we would come back to the city, and would eat at Windows on the World, the iconic restaurant at the top of the North Tower that offered breath-taking views of Manhattan. This was a trip we had made with her brother, Bo, after his graduation. Sadly, this was not to be.

These two events contributed to Lauren's sense of being—or not being—safe in the world. Her close friend from church, Charlotte Rivers, lost her father to cancer not long after Columbine, and in 2002 close friends from school and choir, Caroline Curtiss and Kate Barton, also lost their fathers to cancer. Andy and I decided to forego a trip to Italy with the Bridge Group, and for the remainder of Lauren's middle and high school years declined to travel as a couple without her, hoping to avoid the anxiety she might experience in our absence.

Lauren liked to sing, but we were shocked when, as a pre-teen, she agreed to open the Christmas Eve program at Central with a solo from the church balcony. She sang the first verse of *Once in Royal David's City* a cappella, as it is sung when the Service of Lessons and Carols convenes at King's College in Cambridge, England each year. The church was perfectly silent, and her voice was as clear as a bell. I held my breath until the organ music swelled and the choir began the second verse. It was a proud moment. Shortly thereafter, Lauren auditioned for the Rocky Mountain Children's Choir, where she continued to perform in various community venues through her junior year in high school.

Lauren loved spending time with Grandma Laurie, who shared her passion for art projects and possessed no end of patience and creativity for sewing stuffed animals, drawing greeting cards, and decorating Easter eggs. Lauren and her grandmother were soulmates; they shared a special bond. Laurie mailed homemade chocolate chip cookies, packed in real—not Styrofoam—popcorn to Lauren regularly while she attended Dartmouth College in Hanover, New Hampshire, and one year attended the homecoming game against Harvard and the bonfire afterward, never complaining about the long walks across campus or the stairs at the historic inn where we stayed. The night Laurie died, May 5, 2016, Lauren's sixth sense had her leave in the middle of a coding class she was taking to drive to Sunrise Assisted

Living Center, where her grandmother had moved two years earlier. She surprised Andy, who was already there, and together they waited while aides prepared Laurie for bed. Lauren and Andy held Mom, who seemed to know it was her time, until she quietly passed. Lauren then read aloud to her the last few pages of her unfinished library book, closing a chapter in all our lives.

Lauren was also close to Nana Betty, and attended Nana Camp in Texas during the summer with her Hester cousins—Thomas, Liz, Neil, and Lili. Her Kenney cousins, Kathy and Kris, were old enough to babysit her, which they did, along with several other popular sitters, including Alex's older sister, Lauren. Another favorite was Anjali Nanda, today an immigration attorney with a prominent firm, whose Hindu beliefs influenced Lauren to forego eating meat from the time she was in fifth grade through almost four years of college.

Perhaps because she had such wonderful caregivers herself, Lauren was loving and nurturing toward children, highly in demand as a preferred sitter for the children of our friends and neighbors. At age eleven, she applied to participate in a tutoring partnership between Central Presbyterian Church and Wyman Elementary, stating on her application "I like children and I like reading to them." She was employed to work in the nursery at Central at the age of twelve, after completing the Red Cross babysitting course with other members of her girl scout troop, and, as a teen, began telling stories to children aged three to six in the church's Bible Story Room. This storytelling, using a unique method known as Godly Play, was eventually moved into the sanctuary, and shared with the entire congregation during Central's regular worship service. Lauren continued as one of Central's storytellers while visibly pregnant with Stella, until the Covid pandemic rendered corporate worship unsafe. She recently resumed her storyteller role—Stella sitting with the other children in the first pew and listening intently to her mother.

When considering high schools, we left it to Lauren to select the one that felt right for her. About half of her friends chose to continue in independent schools while the other half transitioned to public schools. After reviewing a wide range of options, she selected Colorado Academy as her first choice. A focus on academic excellence, a broad sampling of visual and performance arts, and a wide range of sports activities for students at all levels of ability were the winning combination. After a year of riding home from school on the CA bus with a group of other ninth graders from our Hilltop neighborhood, playing on the girls' volleyball team, and joining several clubs and organizations—including the Gay/Straight Alliance, Model UN, and Beyond Our Borders, which she co-founded—Lauren had firmly cemented a friendship group that would remain intact through the next four years and beyond. However, the solitary pursuit of writing was still her passion. During her four years at Colorado Academy, she published "Math Wrath" in *A Celebration of Poets* (2002-03), "Pansy" for RTD "Poetry on the Go", and "Top of the Hill" in both *Poetry Patterns* and *Creative Communications*. Her short story, "Southampton", appeared in *The Anthology of Short Stories by Young Americans* (2003). She won CA's Frank Wallace Writing Award her senior year.

Lauren and I took a memorable trip in June of 2004, between her sophomore and junior years at CA. The trip was originally planned with my sister-in-law, Olive, and her daughter, Liz. At the last minute, Liz had a change of plans, so Lauren and I alone flew to St. Louis, Missouri, stayed a night in neighboring St. Charles, then spent two weeks driving to Portland, Oregon. We followed the Missouri River along the route traveled by Meriwether Lewis and William Clark—to whom Olive is distantly related on her father's side—during the bicentennial of the famous Lewis and Clark Expedition of 1804-1806. In addition to visiting the many interpretive centers run by the National Park Service, we visited the Harry S. Truman Presidential

Library, three colleges, and multiple national monuments along the way. I did all the driving, as Lauren was too young to be on a rental agreement, and the GPS technology we were using for the first time sometimes had us going in circles. Our accommodations ranged from cheap hotels to Select Registry Bed and Breakfasts, to rented rooms in private homes. Each twenty-four hours was an adventure, and the scenery was spectacular. On our approach to the home outside Pierre, South Dakota we had reserved for a night, we could see a tornado gathering force on the horizon and moving parallel to us. We barreled over a bumpy road at breakneck speed with no shelter in sight. When we finally reached our destination, we each grabbed a bag and jumped out of the car, breathlessly explaining to our homeowner host we had not had dinner as we followed her down a flight of stairs to an apartment decorated from floor to ceiling in Coca Cola memorabilia. She brought us a plate of cheese, crackers, and salami (Lauren was vegetarian at the time) and retreated upstairs as a deafening clap of thunder shook the house and everything went dark. We spent a stormy night huddled together in bed, but in the morning, we stepped from the walkout basement into a clear sunlit day, and onto the banks of the Missouri, the longest river in the United States.

Just as school was letting out for the summer Lauren had met Jake Van Hook in an art class at CA. During our road trip, his picture was always placed on the nightstand next to her side of the bed. Back in Denver, their romance blossomed, and though he left for Dartmouth College in the fall he soon returned home due to a health issue. Lauren and Jake were inseparable during her junior year and his gap year. He left again in August before her senior year, but Lauren visited him when we took a tour of northeastern colleges that fall. She fell in love with the old and slightly spooky Dartmouth campus, with the immaculate Green as its centerpiece. She visualized herself in the Georgian-style Sanborn Library, paneled and chandelier-lit, where tea and cookies have been served every day between four and five o'clock for generations of Dartmouth students and faculty. Though she visited colleges throughout the country during her last two years of high school—other Ivies, small liberal arts schools, large research universities, Presbyterian-affiliated schools (including Austin College, my father's beloved alma mater)—when the time came, she applied "early action" to Dartmouth, and was accepted. This was the only college application she submitted.

Lauren could not have been more prepared, both academically and emotionally, to leave home for New Hampshire, but we wondered if she was prepared for a New England winter. Whereas Colorado is cold, dry, and sunny, New Hampshire is cold, wet, and overcast. With the help of a couple of SAD (Seasonal Affective Disorder) lamps, she made it through. Upon arrival in Hanover, the three of us set to work scouring her dorm room, which did not appear to have had a thorough cleaning in at least twenty years. Then she decorated it with the accessories she had shipped ahead in the pink and green color palette she chose.

The two young men who lived across the hall from Lauren, Herman Bajwa and Danny Wiebecke, introduced themselves, and became her constant companions for the next four years, attending her wedding in 2017 from Amsterdam and Brooklyn, respectively. Late that first year, the plumbing in the men's bathroom across the hall malfunctioned, sending water under her door and into her room, soaking her belongings. Unfortunately, this was not a one-time event. To add to the stress, her relationship with Jake was on rocky ground, and they broke up at the end of that year. But when Andy flew back with her in the fall of her sophomore year and took her and her friends out for Indian food, he reported there was a new man on the scene, Harrison Taylor, a Canadian from Toronto and a member of the Dartmouth hockey team.

Because she so loved children and learning, we always expected Lauren would become a teacher. But even though she engaged in multiple short-term and volunteer experiences in the field of education, including substitute teaching at St. Anne's, CA, and Escuela de Guadalupe in Denver, her career ambition lay in other areas—sales and marketing. This should not have come as a shock; she was the star salesperson in her scout troop, selling over a thousand boxes of cookies year after year. She kept meticulous records from one season to the next, returning to existing customers for increased sales, and always asking for referrals. She was a natural.

Lauren never had to work hard at getting a job—in fact, jobs seemed to fall into her lap—and she developed faith the right one would always come along. Her high school summer employment included working as secretary at Love Publishing Company, owned by Stan Love, a longtime friend from church, selling jewelry at the Brighton store in the Cherry Creek Mall owned by our across-the-street neighbor, and "nannying" for Jan Bundy down the street and for Stefanie Jones, another good friend from church. Near the end of her senior year at Dartmouth, another good friend from church, Hugh Williamson, a retired CEO who started the book club Andy belongs to, asked at their monthly meeting what Lauren would be doing after graduation. Andy replied he thought she would be coming back to Denver to look for a job. Hugh replied, "Well I'll give her a job, just have her call me."

We attended graduation on June 13, 2010, where Lauren walked across the stage to receive her diploma from Dr. Jim Kim, President of Dartmouth College at the time, a pediatrician who had earlier co-founded Partners in Health with Dr. Paul Farmer, and who later became president of the World Bank. Lauren was awarded a Bachelor of Arts degree with emphases in English and creative writing, and had received multiple honorable citations during her four years. After the ceremony, we enjoyed a celebratory brunch with the Taylor family, and then began to pack up the Volvo sedan that Lauren and Harry had brought to Hanover from Denver over their spring break for her drive home. There were tearful goodbyes—to Harry, her boyfriend of three years who she would not see again per their mutual agreement—to Herman and Danny, and to Kathleen and Rebecca, Kappa sisters and future bridesmaids.

After dropping Andy at the Manchester airport sixty miles south-east of Hanover, Lauren and I continued toward Denver, meandering through the beautiful fields of Virginia and Pennsylvania with the Dixie Chicks blaring, toward Laurens County, South Carolina, where I planned to look at a mansion for sale. I had always wanted to own a bed and breakfast, to Andy's chagrin, and thought this six-bedroom house in the town where Presbyterian College was located might be a prospect. In the end the property would have required too much work for even my talented architect husband, but Lauren and I had lots of fun imagining the possibilities.

Back in Denver, Lauren rented and decorated her first apartment in Wheat Ridge and reported for work at XeDAR, the geo-spatial mapping company Hugh ran in Arvada. She described her job to us as "copy girl", but a year and a half later, when the company was purchased by a large public corporation, IHS, she worked personally with Hugh to rebrand the acquired entity. She then chose to resign from the company and continue under a contract arrangement, hoping to broaden her experience while enjoying more flexibility. The business card she printed read "Lauren E. Kenney, Creative Consultant & Technical Writer".

Freelancing was difficult, as the country continued to recover from the recession of 2008. Lauren moved back in with us for a while, an arrangement I was unhappy about. I felt concerned she was going backward and was impatient for her to find another "real job", one with health insurance and a retirement plan. Never mind the fact that she was substitute teaching in addition to her contract work and required nominal financial help, I felt embarrassed when friends asked about her, even though the basements of middle-class America were full of adult children with college degrees during those years. Thankfully Lauren was able to stay positive and be the adult during this period, because I behaved like a selfish child. Before long she found a job with Iron-Point Marketing, a start-up company that integrated sales and marketing platforms. There she met one of her closest friends and future bridesmaids, Kendall Wilson.

A word about the Dartmouth diploma: it is written entirely in Latin, and Lauren's features a gold seal stamped with the Cum Laude designation. Any college education is dear, but unlike other excellent colleges and universities, the Ivy League schools offer no merit-based aid. I am fortunate to be able to say we did not qualify for financial aid. Lauren's education was funded with a combination of tax-deferred college savings plans established by my parents and by us, her summer jobs, her part-time employment with the Dartmouth Alumni Association making calls for contributions, a National Merit scholarship sponsored by MetLife, and a Robert C. Byrd education award. Lauren graduated from college with no debt. When we had her diploma framed and presented it to her on her twenty-third birthday, I fully and naively expected her to hang it in her cubicle at XeDAR, a suggestion that produced a visible rolling of eyes. My next idea was to hang it over the mantelpiece in our living room, reasoning that it represented a much larger investment than any art we will ever own. Today, however, Lauren's diploma hangs in her former upstairs bedroom, where Stella now sleeps when she spends the night with Nana and Papa.

During the freelancing time, Lauren was—as always—writing, and one of her genres was poetry she put to a beat. She rapped at open mics in LoDo (Lower Downtown) and RiNo (River North) bars for weeks before I asked to go with her. When I did, I was amazed at her talent, clearly appreciated by others as well. The love of language and beat, including rap and hip-hop, turned out to be a connection between Lauren and Alex—but that comes later. Lauren is a Four on the Enneagram chart—creative and unique, expressing her own identity, seeking relationships while at times seeming remote in a group setting. I was inept at understanding her as a child, and sought guidance from friends, psychologists, and stacks of self-help library books. I wanted her to be the version of myself I wished I were, and she had a strong and willful desire to be herself. Thank goodness she prevailed.

Photos

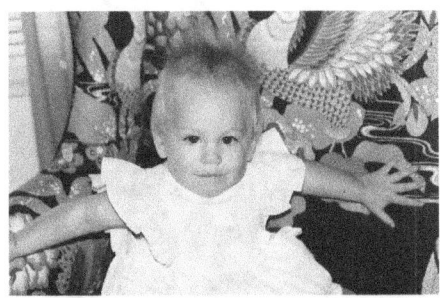

Lauren and her "ecstatic" hair

Lauren and Bo, w/
Rev. John Wilcox and Sue

Lauren and Lauren—
future sisters-in-law

"On my honor..."

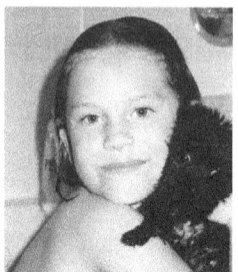

Lauren and Inky

Lauren and Hester cousins Wyatt,
Lili, Liz and Neil

St. Anne's graduation, w/Ms. Stockdale

The fateful Mexico jellyfish trip

Sweet Sixteen, w/Andy and
Grandma Laurie

Colorado Academy rising senior

Receiving the Dartmouth diploma

*Lauren and bridesmaids Rebecca,
Kendall, Kathleen, Lauren,
and Kristen*

Barbara Lee Beard Berv

Baba

BARBARA LEE BEARD BERV, or *Baba*, as her older grandchildren previously named her, grew up in the University Hills neighborhood of Denver, the youngest of three children born to Glynn Allen and Gertrude Juliana Brul Beard. Gertrude was the youngest of eight children, and her mother, Barbara's maternal grandmother, Juliana Bridgett Popp Brul, was forty-five years old when she was born. Gertrude's father, Carl Ludwig Brul, who had changed the family name from Bruhl to Brul prior to her birth, referred to his little daughter as his "harvest rose", by all accounts a fitting term of endearment. Gertrude was born in Altenburg, Missouri, but when she was five years old her parents moved the family to Colorado, first to Spring Valley, where they stayed only a few weeks, and then to La Junta. Gertrude was a voracious reader from a young age, a passion she passed down to Barbara, who has been in a book group for over forty years.

Glynn Beard ran his own successful pharmaceutical distribution business, which included a drug he patented in 1967 named Nylorac (Carolyn, his oldest child's name, spelled backward), an analgesic tablet containing acetaminophen. He had grown up poor in Garden

City, Missouri, and after attending a year of college joined the Civilian Conservation Corps, a public works program that employed millions of men to work on environmental projects during the Great Depression. When the United States entered World War II, Glynn enlisted in the Army and became a medical assistant. This experience, no doubt, contributed to his choice of career when the war ended. Glynn was charming and outgoing, and a good salesman. His clients, who often became his friends, were medical doctors. Glynn and Gertrude enjoyed opera outings with them and their wives, and the men played golf together.

Barbara's siblings were Carolyn Ruth, born September 8, 1944, and John Allen, born May 22, 1946. Gertrude had miscarried a third child before becoming pregnant again and giving birth to Barbara on April 22, 1950, at age thirty-four. Gertrude grew up in the Lutheran church, but Glynn's family was originally from Scotland, where the Presbyterian denomination originated, and he had been reared in that faith tradition. The family was active at Wellshire Presbyterian Church, conveniently located near the Beards' home. Gertrude, who never drove, could walk to the church to participate in Bible study and volunteer work with other members of her Presbyterian Women's circle.

Glynn often invited people he met at church in the morning to Sunday dinner later that same afternoon, and Barbara tells of hosting guests from Russia, India, Cuba, and Hungary in her family's home. Her father was interested in and accepting of people from all walks of life. He once observed that during the war he had given shots to Blacks and other persons of color, and that they all bled the same red blood.

Like many men of his generation coming home from the second world war, Glynn developed a dependency on alcohol. It did not seem to affect his work or his friendships, but it affected his family relationships. His son John left home to join the Navy immediately after high school graduation, in part to distance himself from his father, and Gertrude made the decision to leave Glynn around the time of Barbara's first pregnancy in 1978. Glynn died six years later. Barbara and her siblings remained close to their mother until her death.

Barbara attended Bradley Elementary, the neighborhood school located near her family's home. In the fifties, children's assigned seats in the classroom were often arranged alphabetically, and Barbara Beard and Jan Berne were placed next to each other at age seven, the beginning of a close friendship that continues today. Both girls shared an aptitude for academics that landed them in accelerated classes in grade school and advanced placement classes throughout their six years at Thomas Jefferson, the combined middle and high school they attended.

As teenagers, neither Barbara nor Jan had much interest in dating, preferring to keep each other company over the weekend, enjoying sleepovers and playing Monopoly and other board games. Barbara smoked a few cigarettes, and the girls both discovered vodka gimlets, thanks to Carolyn. Both worked after school and during the summer months for spending money and college savings. They graduated from TJ, as it is affectionately known in Denver, in 1968. Jan received a scholarship to the University of Denver, and Barbara enrolled at Colorado State University in Fort Collins. Her parents would not allow her to attend the University of Colorado, concerned there were "too many hippies" in Boulder, and DU and Colorado College, in Colorado Springs, were too expensive.

Barbara majored in English and French, and was awarded a Bachelor of Arts degree from CSU in June of 1972. She immediately earned a secondary education teaching certificate, but at that point the high enrollment numbers of the baby boom had subsided, and classroom teaching jobs were hard to come by. Her first full-time job out of college was selling the services of a collection agency, where she was successful at bringing in new accounts, but often worried about the people on the receiving end of the services she was selling. In 1973, Barbara went to work as a service representative for Mountain Bell, located in downtown Denver, where she would remain for twelve years, advancing after two years to supervisor, and then to manager.

Barbara met Dan Berv at a party she attended during the summer of 1974. He flirted openly with her, but Jan, also at the party, warned Barbara to avoid Dan, describing him as a wild man—divorced, with a child—with whom she probably did not want to get involved. Despite Barbara's attempts to follow her friend's advice, Dan pursued her in ludicrous ways, riding his bike past her apartment as she was returning from work and feigning surprise at running into her. His persistence paid off, and in a short while they were dating. The fact that Dan had a child became a plus in Barbara's mind; six-year-old Damion was so engaging she had to assume his father was doing a good job of parenting.

Sometimes an event occurs in a person's life, so pivotal that every other event seems to occur in juxtaposition to it. So it was for Dan Berv, and by association for Barbara, on October 18, two months into their courtship, when the apartment he lived in at 10 South Sherman Street erupted in flames, likely from a cigarette left smoldering on a piece of upholstered furniture. Unable to escape his third-floor unit through the door, Dan jumped from a window, where the heat had melted the aluminum casing. The windshield of a car parked below broke his fall. Jan heard on a radio news show that Dan had been taken by ambulance to Denver General—now Denver Health—then, as now, one of the top trauma hospitals in the country. She called Barbara, who left work and rushed to the hospital. From that point on, when Barbara was not at work, she was at Dan's side. Ten surgeries and eleven months later, on September 20, 1975, they were married at Wellshire Presbyterian Church.

In December of 1978, Barbara gave birth to a daughter, Lauren, and in September of 1982, to Alex. Mountain Bell allowed generous parental leave for each birth, but with three children—Damion was now living with the family—full-time work was more challenging. In 1983, at which point she had ultimate responsibility for sixty-five supervisors and service reps, Barbara took advantage of a buyout offer presented by US West, the successor entity of Mountain Bell after its divestiture from AT&T, that was equal to one year's salary and benefits.

That same year, I met Jan Netting, née Berne. I was an agent for Great-West Life Assurance Company, a Canadian company that had recently moved its United States headquarters to Denver, while Jan, a paralegal, worked in the Advanced Sales department. We were among a handful of women with the company, and naturally sought one another's friendship and support. Jan had three-year old fraternal twins, Eric and Matthew, and needed the break from parenting that work provided. We officed in the Great-West Life Tower at the corner of Broadway and 17th Street, referred to in Denver circles at that time as Wall Street of the West.

Jan talked about her best friend from childhood, Barbara, and her husband, Dan, a successful executive, and president of Imperial Headwear. (Jan never mentioned her earlier concerns about Dan to me!) When the Bervs decided to move from their Mayfair home to a larger one in Hilltop, the Nettings suggested that Tom, my husband at that time, and I might be interested in purchasing it. I remember touring the home and observing that Damion and my son Bo, born within six months of each other, appeared to share a mutual interest in "heavy metal". Black Sabbath, Metallica, and Iron Maiden posters decorated the walls of his bedroom.

Once the Berv family settled into their new home at 60 Cherry Street, Barbara began to think about returning to work. Though Dan's income was more than adequate for the family's needs, she missed having a schedule and interacting with professional colleagues. Her segue into the non-profit world began with a volunteer position. A friend of Jan's husband Rob was married to a woman who worked for Special Olympics, and after hearing about Barbara from Rob, invited Barbara to become involved. Barbara's excellent management and marketing skills did not go unnoticed, and a year later she was in the paid position of Volunteer Coordinator. When Barbara left the organization two years later, it utilized a volunteer management system she had created.

Barbara was still with Special Olympics in 1988 when Dan lost his job at Imperial. He had begun to lay the groundwork for his own manufacturing company, and the word inadvertently got out. Denver was in the second year of the oil shale bust—not an ideal time to start a new business. For a while, Dan worked for a company in Scottsdale that made customized towels, head covers, and other promotional materials for golf club pro shops around the country. He even considered moving his family to Arizona, but ultimately decided to start the business he had planned, Headline Sports, in Denver, regardless of the shaky economy.

Jan and I were now officing with Great-West Life in Greenwood Village, on the tenth floor of one of three beautiful new office towers the company had constructed to accommodate its growing business. Tom and I had divorced, and I was married to Andy Kenney. We had a daughter, Lauren, born in August of 1987. We had met the Bervs but were not really friends with them yet.

Meanwhile Barbara had been recruited to develop and lead the Young Americans Education Foundation, non-profit arm of the Young Americans Bank. YAB was the brainchild of Denver cable pioneer Bill Daniels—a bank for customers under the age of twenty-one, personally backed by him. The goal of both the bank and the foundation was financial literacy for young people, allowing them to become responsible citizens and full participants in America's free enterprise system. Barbara's business acumen, and her interests in young people and education, made her the perfect candidate for this new role, which she held for nine years.

In the fall of 1993, Rob Netting suggested that Lauren Berv, almost fifteen years old, would be an ideal babysitter for our Lauren, who had just turned six. We had moved back to our Cherry Creek condominium on South Garfield while our new 1938-era home on Albion Street was being remodeled—just five minutes southwest of the Bervs' home on Cherry Street—so the arrangements were easily made. Less than a year later we were back in Hilltop, just three doors down from Steck Elementary School, which shares a campus with Hill Middle School, where Alex Berv would attend the following year.

Sometime during the nineties—none of us can remember exactly when—Jan observed that she and Barbara and I had all been born within months of each other and should form a birthday club. She invited Nancy Sharpe, another friend from Great-West Life, to join us. During the years leading up to our fiftieth, and for two decades after, the four of us enjoyed regularly scheduled celebratory lunches and "happy hours". We traveled together on milestone birthdays. We still celebrate (and sometimes commiserate) life—together. Dede Pahl joined us along the way, and we now see Nancy infrequently. Her husband, George, died in 2018, and there is a new love in her life, for which we are all happy. And to be honest, the current toxic political environment is a factor. Nancy is an elected official, deeply involved in politics, and on the opposite side of the aisle from the rest of us.

Headline Sports became a successful enterprise—so successful, in fact, that in 1999, after having left her job at the bank, Barbara began assisting Dan in sales and marketing for the company. She did this work for two years and discovered, as many have, that working with one's spouse is not always the best arrangement. There were other stresses for her during this period as well. Gertrude was aging and developing dementia, and Carolyn, who had been diagnosed with MS years earlier, was worsening.

With these personal demands, there was little time for Barbara to proactively look for meaningful work. But in 2002 she heard about an opening for Senior Philanthropic Advisor at The Denver Foundation, and she applied. She got the job, and her circle of influence and contacts continued to expand. She and I saw each other more often now, as the foundation was a consistent provider of quality continuing education for estate planning professionals, which included financial planners.

On November 20, 2002, Gertrude Beard died. Friends and family members spoke lovingly of her at her memorial service, which I attended, at Celebration Community Church. Barbara's sister and brother were there. Now they too have passed, and Barbara's story would not be complete without a word about both.

Carolyn, the first-born child of Glynn and Gertrude Beard, was a typical "oldest" and had a reputation with her younger siblings for being "the boss". She worked for many years at Colorado National Bank, which she jokingly referred to as Colorado Bashional Nank, playing a word game introduced by Gertrude to her children and grandchildren. Carolyn married Andrew Shaw, and became full-time mother to his children, Lonnie and Stephanie, whom she adopted, and loved dearly. She also provided many hours of care for Damion, and for Lauren, while Barbara worked. Her nephews and nieces, including Jeanna, John's daughter—who loved visiting Uncle Andy and Aunt Carolyn—describe her as being lots of fun. Sadly, Stephanie died in her early twenties. Lonnie has left the Denver area. Both children suffered emotional scars from their early childhood.

Around the age of thirty-five Carolyn was diagnosed with multiple sclerosis. Although the disease is potentially debilitating, Carolyn refused to be defined by it, and continued to live an active and independent life. Several years later her husband was diagnosed with cancer; he died while the children were still in their teens. Eventually Carolyn moved into the same apartment building her mother now lived in, and the two cared for each other and kept each other company until each required additional assistance.

Carolyn was active with other family members at Corona Presbyterian, and then at Celebration Community Church, where she taught Sunday school and Vacation Bible School, and worked with refugee children who attended nearby Ellis Elementary. Her final residence was Brookshire House Rehabilitation and Care Community, where she lived for over ten years. While there, Carolyn was active on the Residents' Council, at one point serving as its elected president. Prior to her time in leadership, it was common practice for the staff at the center to move the wheelchair-bound residents around as if they were pieces of furniture. Carolyn introduced and advocated for a rule that required the staff to first speak with a resident and obtain his or her permission to be moved—a simple but meaningful act of respect.

Another Brookshire resident, David Haight, who also had MS, became Carolyn's close friend and constant companion. The two of them enjoyed going out or just staying in to watch public television. They attended David's church together on Sunday evenings until he died in 2013. Carolyn continued to attend her own church on Sunday mornings until a year prior to her death, maneuvering her electric wheelchair over ice and snow on the coldest winter days. She died on December 28, 2014. Everyone who knew her speaks of her positive attitude and her strength of character.

While stationed in Japan early in his naval career, John—Barbara's older and Carolyn's younger brother—met and married Yoshiko

Masuda. The couple had three children—James Michael (JM), born October 9, 1971, Jeffery Daniel (Jeffy) born September 3, 1973, and Jeanna Catherine, born September 10, 1985. They settled in Maryland, where John completed twenty-one years with the Navy. After his military retirement he went to work as a cryptologist for the National Security Administration, where he won numerous honors. Jeanna once asked her father about his work for a fourth-grade assignment, and he jokingly told her, "If I tell you, I'll have to kill you." John loved dogs, and the family had many canine friends over the years. His favorite was Tuffy. Jeanna told me she saw her father cry two times. The first was when Tuffy died. The second was when he brought Jeanna to Colorado in 2001 to see the Olympic Training Center in Colorado Springs, and they visited his mother in Denver. Gertrude didn't seem to know her son during the visit, but as he and Jeanna turned to leave, she said "Johnny?". Jeanna herself becomes tearful remembering her father, who died of cardiac arrest at the age of fifty-eight—having just received a major promotion—when she was only eighteen years old.

I asked Jeanna if her father had continued in the Presbyterian faith of his childhood; she responded that neither he nor her mother considered themselves to be religious. However, for Japanese people, both Buddhism and Shintoism play a spiritual as well as a cultural role, and Yoshiko continues a beautiful and meaningful tradition that Jeanna described to me. When she travels to Japan for family visits, Yoshiko goes to the graves of her parents. She cleans the surrounding area, washes their headstones, places fresh flowers, lights a candle or incense, and says a few words of gratitude for their lives and a prayer for their souls. She carries out this same tradition at the Maryland Military Cemetery in Crownsville, where John was laid to rest in 2004. Sometimes Jeanna goes with her mother, but it makes her sad, because she misses her father so much.

JM followed in his father's footsteps and joined the Navy at age seventeen. Jeffery started college in South Carolina on a baseball scholarship but returned to the University of Maryland, Baltimore County after a sports injury, where he met and married Nicole. Together they have Reagan, Reese, and Rylan, Stella's second cousins. Jeanna also graduated from UMBC, with a degree in Environmental Science; she received her master's degree in Environmental Management at Loughborough University, in England.

Jeanna wanted a team sport in college, and chose rugby over soccer, field hockey, and lacrosse. The last semester of her senior year she met her husband-to-be, Kevin Mann, playing club rugby in Annapolis. He was two years older than she and had earned degrees in physics and education at Lock Haven University in Pennsylvania. The couple became engaged at Christmas in 2012 and moved to Denver, where Kevin teaches high school physics in the Cherry Creek School District and Jeanna works for the Colorado Department of Public Health and Environment as an air pollution inspector, with responsibility over multiple counties. They have been married since 2014 and are parents to an English bulldog named Melonpan, and a yellow Labrador (mix) named Yumi. They are well known on the rugby scene: Jeanna plays for the Colorado Gray Wolves and coaches the Colorado Rush, an inclusive men's team, and Kevin plays for the Denver Waterdogs. Barbara is proud of them both, and organized a group of friends and family last summer to attend one of Jeanna's games. She is thrilled to have her niece living near her, and is excitedly looking forward to having Jeff, Jeanna's brother, and his family in Denver for the upcoming Thanksgiving holiday. Holiday dinners at the Berv home are legend—well over twenty guests at times—and there always seems to be room for one more. Butler Rents, Denver's go-to provider for entertainment needs, keeps a standard order on file for Barbara.

To her siblings, Barbara was "Barbie", but she prefers to be called Barbara. "After all," her mother once told her, "Barbara is the name I gave you." Barbara is also a more fitting name for the professional positions she continued to be promoted to. It should be noted here that although Barbara worked throughout her childrearing years, she somehow found time to volunteer at each of the children's schools, serving as co-president of the Parent Teacher Association at Hill Middle School when Lauren attended there, and continuing on as a PTA officer at Manual High School. She was also active in PTA roles when Alex attended Carson Elementary and Hill.

Linda Childears, retired President and Chief Executive Officer of the Daniels Fund, was President and CEO of the Young Americans Bank when Barbara became involved with it, remaining in that role until 2005, at which time she was also serving on the board of directors of the Denver Public Schools Foundation. Michael Bennet, today one of Colorado's two U.S. senators, was the superintendent of DPS, and in 2005, the foundation was seeking a CEO. Linda, who had mentored Barbara at the bank, immediately thought of her former colleague for the job, and Barbara was recruited. Having previously demonstrated her strong support for the Denver Public School system and for public education in general, Barbara was thrilled. At a recent Bennet fundraiser that Andy and I attended, I mentioned to him that Barbara and I now share a granddaughter. He remembered her with warmth and expansive praise, a common reaction whenever Barbara's name is mentioned.

From the DPS Foundation, Barbara returned to The Denver Foundation, this time in the role of Vice-President of Philanthropic Services. When I retired from my financial planning career a year later, in 2010, Barbara was interviewing candidates to connect with professional advisors—attorneys, accountants, and financial planners. I thought this would be the perfect second career for me, so I applied.

Barbara made it clear she would not hire a friend—a wise decision for which I have thanked her.

Though Barbara retired from The Denver Foundation in 2016, her expertise remains in high demand, and she has since worked on a consulting basis for Canopy Advisory Group's non-profit division, assisting clients such as Urban Peak, and our church—Central Presbyterian—with their strategic development goals. Through another connection she consults with the Kirkland Museum. Sometimes, when we are out together, it seems Barbara knows everyone in Denver. Her work has touched many lives.

Barbara is the heart of her family, not just because she *has* such a big heart, but because it is she who continues to gather its members together—for holidays, birthdays, and other celebrations, and for memorial events. Jeanna and Kevin are included as her own children on these occasions, and Vera Berv, her former sister-in-law, as her own sister. Andy and I are also treated like family. Though her older grandchildren, Penny and Teddy, have never lived in Denver, *Baba* read to them using FaceTime when they were younger, a practice she continued with Damion's son Danny, who lives north of Denver, in Thornton. Barbara marvels at Stella's every new development, seeing this grandchild more frequently than the others. I marvel at my good fortune in having such a wonderful friend with which to share grandparenting.

Photos

Barbara's mother, Gertrude Brul, her father's "harvest rose"

Brul siblings—Gertrude and George (front), Elsie, Hugo, Hilda, Paula, Rudolph, and Lydia (back)

Barbara's grandmother—Juliana Brul

Barbara's father, Glynn Beard

Barbara and her siblings

Barbara and her children

Barbara and Jan

John and Yoshiko Beard, JM and Jeff

John and Jeanna

Jeff and Nicole Beard

Jeanna Beard and Kevin Mann,
Yumi and Melonpan

Dede, Sherry, Barbara, Jan,
Nancy—the birthday group

Daniel Alexander Berv

Pops

DAN BERV HAS ENJOYED success as both a corporate executive and an entrepreneur. Today he is an accomplished artist—self-taught—whose vibrant acrylic paintings sell almost as fast as he can complete them. He is a master griller, and an enthusiastic gardener. He was an avid long-distance runner for over thirty years, but finally had to give that up due to a complaining back. Now he walks daily, either with his wife, Barbara, or with his primary care physician and close friend, Dan Citron. Dan Berv is a gentleman, a gentle man—the kind who writes a personal thank-you note the day after you have hosted a dinner party. He is a devoted husband, father, and grandfather. So, when I told him I wanted to interview him for my book, to learn more about his branch of Stella's family tree, I was surprised at his initial response—that he didn't want to talk about it. "You can read about my dad on the internet", he said. "Just "google" the Berv brothers", Barbara suggested. So that's how I began.

Dan's father, Arthur, was born in 1906 in Warsaw, Poland, to Samuel Borovokunkin (or Berwikunkin—there are variations on the name), a Talmudic scholar who had emigrated there from Belarus, and Pearl Newmark, the sophisticated woman who married Samuel (after breaking off another engagement) and introduced him into her cultured society. Arthur had an older brother, Henry, and would have two younger brothers, Jack, and Harry. Prior to Harry's birth, Samuel and Pearl immigrated to the United States with their three boys. At Ellis Island, on the way to their new home in New Brunswick, New Jersey, the family name was shortened to Berv. Lauren and Alex found the record of his great-grandparents' passage when visiting the Statue of Liberty shortly after they were married.

Harry, the youngest of the four Berv brothers and the only one born in the United States, developed respiratory problems, and his parents moved their family from New Jersey to Chisholm, Minnesota, a small mining town known for its clean mountain air. There, in school, the boys all demonstrated musical aptitude, and their music teacher started each of them on a different instrument: Henry on violin, Arthur on trumpet, Jack on cello, and Harry on piano. Before long he told the boys' parents that he had taught them all he could. He encouraged them to move to Philadelphia—at that time considered to be the center for classical music in the United States—which they did. Samuel eventually owned a general store in that city.

In Philadelphia, Arthur changed instruments, from trumpet to French horn, and became assistant to the Principal Horn in the Philadelphia Orchestra. At the age of fifteen he was named Principal Horn, under music director Leopold Stokowski, keeping a schedule that made it impossible for him to graduate from high school. He later received an honorary degree.

In 1937, the NBC Symphony Orchestra was formed in New York City. This was a radio orchestra, the brainchild of David Sarnoff, the president of Radio Broadcasting Corporation, created especially for the conductor Arturo Toscanini, who had recently resigned from the New York Philharmonic and returned to his home in Italy. Sarnoff sent an emissary, Samuel Chotzinoff, to convince Toscanini to return, and hired a well-known orchestra builder, Artur Rodzinski, to recruit the best classical musicians in the country. Arthur, now playing under Eugene Ormandy, was hired as Principal Horn, quadrupling his income with one career move. Jack and Harry—who were now also hornists—were hired as second and third. Toscanini was known for lashing out at his musicians, but he treated his top hornists with respect, understanding that if he lost one, he would lose all three.

The oldest Berv brother, Henry, continued as a professional violinist. He married a Parisian woman and settled in France. But the three youngest brothers remained with the NBC Symphony until Toscanini retired in the spring of 1954, continuing for a time with its successor orchestra, Symphony of the Air. They also free-lanced, dominating the New York horn world; their artistry is referred to as "the Berv sound" in music literature. In the fall of 1954 the original *Tonight Show*, co-created and hosted by Steve Allen, aired on NBC. Skitch Henderson conducted the show's orchestra, comprised of incredibly talented jazz and classical musicians. Arthur was on French horn.

All three hornist brothers taught - Arthur at Manhattan School of Music, Jack at Yale, and Harry at Julliard—and all eventually became studio musicians, playing for Broadway shows and cinema soundtracks. The theme song from the popular NBC documentary series *Victory at Sea*, which won an Emmy Award in 1954, featured Arthur, as did the original Star Trek television theme song. But according to Dan, his father—a child prodigy and true virtuoso—loved classical music, and anything that came after that he viewed as a comedown.

In 1940, Arthur married Suzanne Sidney Goldberg, an artist— also professionally trained to perform opera—who had studied at the University of New Mexico and at the Sorbonne. They had two sons, Elliott James, born April 30, 1943, and Daniel Alexander, born April 6, 1946. Elliott's middle name comes from Suzanne's brother. Dan's name has no known family significance, but there is a funny story. Originally named Alexander Daniel, his name was crossed out and changed to Daniel Alexander on his birth certificate hours after he was born, at the suggestion of Suzanne's mother.

After the war, during which Arthur was stationed in London and played with the United States Army Air Forces Band, the family resided in Forest Hills, in the borough of Queens, and then in Great Neck, on Long Island. Arthur commuted sixteen miles into the city by train for his regular week-night performances. Suzanne gave up singing but continued to create beautiful paintings in a makeshift studio in the basement of their home, and beautiful gardens outside. She was once interviewed by *The New York Times* about the prize bonsai trees she expertly cultivated in the family conservatory. On many Saturday nights, Suzanne and the two boys went into the city for Arthur's concerts at iconic Carnegie Hall, where Dan and his brother met some of the world's finest musicians.

As charmed as their life appeared, it could be painful. Suzanne and Arthur subscribed to a child-rearing methodology proven over time to be ineffective at best, and physically and psychologically harmful at worst. Elliott did his best to protect his younger brother, but after graduating from Great Neck South High School in 1960 he was eager to leave home. He went off to Allegheny College, a highly selective liberal arts school located in Meadville, Pennsylvania, leaving Dan to fend for himself.

Dan tried to stay out of his parents' crosshairs, studying hard and earning good grades, and participating in student government. He ran cross-country and was on his school's soccer and baseball teams. He worked part-time during the school year, and at multiple jobs over the summer. He had his own lawn mowing business, delivered papers, and bussed tables at a local restaurant. He valet-parked cars and tended to sleek boats anchored in the marina at the Port Washington Yacht Club during their owners' absences. There he received full pool and restaurant privileges. He met and dated some very pretty girls.

Like Elliott, Dan left home as soon as he could, enrolling at the University of Cincinnati, which turned out to be less demanding than the high school he and his brother had attended. After a year there he transferred to New York University. One of Dan's favorite memories of growing up was sitting with the band during The Steve Allen Show, next to famous jazz drummer Don Lamond. Dan took up drums himself, and during his college years played in several bands, performing in coffee houses and bars in Greenwich Village, across Washington Square Park from the NYU campus. He considered becoming a professional musician, but decided to pursue business instead, capitalizing on the relationship between musical accomplishment and mathematical prowess. That decision has served Dan well.

While at NYU, Dan met Faune Yerby, daughter of well-known author Frank Yerby and herself a published poet. After graduation they married, and had a son, Damion Alexander, born May 22, 1968. When Damion was a toddler Faune convinced Dan they should leave New York, and suggested Denver as a possible destination. Dan had traveled by train to attend Camp Cheley, located near Estes Park, for several eight-week sessions as a youth, so he knew the allure of the Colorado Rockies. He arrived with his wife and three-year-old son in Denver on July 2, 1971, a year prior to the release of John Denver's hit album and single, *Rocky Mountain High*.

Meanwhile, Elliott had married his high school girlfriend, Vera Dattner, a beautiful girl who graduated one year after he did and began college at Ohio State University. She completed her degree at Miami University of Ohio when Elliott began work there on a master's degree in industrial psychology. Elliott and Vera went about establishing their careers. They moved from Ohio to New York—where Vera obtained a master's degree in speech pathology—to Pennsylvania, Connecticut, and finally Maine. They reared three sons, David (born a year before Damion), Jason, and Peter.

Despite the lack of a close bond with his parents, Dan adored his maternal grandparents, Leo and Barbara Goldberg, who showered him with love and affection whenever he visited them. Leo grew up in Hutchinson, Kansas. He graduated from the Colorado School of Mines, but went to work for Northwestern Mutual Life after marrying Barbara, a younger woman who expressed her preference for a lifestyle that involved more income than a career geologist might typically provide. He became a leading sales agent for the Kansas City, Missouri office of NML, regularly receiving top honors for the number of policies sold in a calendar year. In addition to their daughter, Suzanne, Leo and Barbara had a son, James—Uncle Jimmy to Elliott and Dan—who predeceased his parents. He and his wife and two children lived in Beverly Hills, where he worked in the motion picture business. As a young Jewish man starting out in entertainment, he experienced such discrimination that he quickly changed his last name from Goldberg to Greer.

Leo and Barbara moved from Kansas City to Palm Springs, California, where Leo maintained his insurance business on a limited basis from a home office. Everyone who knew Leo liked him. He and Barbara played golf and bridge, and entered and won numerous Arthur Murray dance competitions held around the country. They remained active until Leo's death in 1980 at the age of ninety-two, after which Barbara lived on for almost a decade. Grandma and Gramps, as they were known, welcomed visits from their grandchildren and great-grandchildren, who loved relaxing by the pool at their desert home. Their long-time housekeeper and beloved companion, Lavalle, would cook up a storm on these occasions—platters of fried chicken, and a wonderful German chocolate cake. But everyone in the family agrees that Lavalle's huge heavenly hugs were the best thing about her.

Two and a half years after moving to Denver, Dan and his first wife divorced, and the following year he met Barbara Beard. Dan was garaging his bike at the home of a friend from work. The friend's roommate, Rob Netting, had dated Barbara's best friend, Jan Berne. There was a party at the friend's house that summer of 1974, and though Jan and Rob had broken up and were currently dating other people, Jan suggested to Barbara that they attend it. Dan was also there, hanging out and playing a set of Conga drums. He met Barbara and was immediately smitten. Jan advised her friend against getting involved with Dan, describing him as too "wild and crazy". But Dan persisted. His son Damion, who Barbara loved the minute she met him, was an added attraction. Barbara and Dan were married in the fall of 1975.

The Berv family expanded when Barbara gave birth to Lauren Michelle on December 17, 1978, and to Alex Richard on September 4, 1982. Alex's middle name comes from Dan's best friend from high school, Richard Algozini, who had also attended business school at NYU, on a full academic scholarship. Richard followed Dan to Denver, passed the CPA exam, and worked as an accountant at Johns Manville before dying from lupus at the young age of thirty-seven.

Dan's business career was on the fast track in 1982 when, after serving as general manager of Imperial Headwear, he became president of the company. Founded in Denver, Imperial had been in continuous operation since 1906, and by the late nineteen-eighties manufactured seventy percent of the ball caps and visors sold in the United States, many of them branded for exclusive country clubs and golf courses, sports teams, and tournaments. It was a balancing act—satisfying an absentee owner who fancied himself a consultant, relating to a factory full of workers of many ethnicities, and negotiating with the union bosses who represented them—but Dan had excellent people skills. He also understood manufacturing and distribution.

Increasingly he saw the benefits of owning his own company. In 1990, after leaving Imperial, and after a brief stint working for a manufacturer in Scottsdale, Arizona, Dan incorporated Headline Sports in north Denver, near Westminster, specializing in screen-printed and embroidered shirts and other promotional products. While in high school Alex worked as an office assistant in his father's company. He also worked in the warehouse, lifting and loading heavy cartons of goods. This was one of his favorite jobs, and perhaps the origin of how he got to be so buff!

When Dan was growing up, his parents practiced Reform Judaism, and attended services at Temple Beth-El with their sons, who were both confirmed at the traditional age of thirteen. During Dan's recovery from the fire that almost took his life in 1974, he became aware of the healing power of prayer. His physical therapist at Denver General Hospital, Bob Gillespie—who Dan describes as an "angel"—debrided his wounded feet and badly burned body twice each day in a whirlpool, and spoke quietly about Jesus Christ. Dan began to think about religion, and about his own faith, something he had not done in many years.

When Barbara's mother transferred her membership from Wellshire to Corona Presbyterian Church, she invited Barbara and Dan and their children to join her there. In 1984 Dan publicly professed his faith, and was baptized in the swimming pool of fellow congregant Jerry McHugh, who lived near the church in the Denver Country Club neighborhood. During this time the Bervs grew close to their youth pastor, Steve Garcia, and when he left Corona to start Celebration Community Church, they, Gertrude, and Barbara's sister, Carolyn, followed him as charter members. There Dan has shared his musical gifts with the congregation, playing drums in the church's praise band. He has also served as an ordained deacon. The current pastor of this very special church closes each worship service with this benediction: "So as you leave this place, take the hand of your savior and the hand of a friend, and in the name of our savior, celebrate."

While at Imperial, Dan became good friends with Bradley Stevens, a CPA working for the company's outside accounting firm. Brad soon left that firm to establish his own, Stevens & Associates. Brad had worked in the tax department at Haskins & Sells with my former husband, Tom, and in addition to becoming my client was one of my oldest and dearest friends in Denver. He died in 2014, several years after a freak accident in which a rock thrown from a landscape company's truck crashed through his front windshield, shattering part of his skull and rendering him blind. He spent months in recovery at Denver General, as had Dan forty years earlier. Andy and I, and Dan, Barbara and Alex, all attended Brad's memorial service. This shared friendship was another of the many ways our two families' paths crossed over the years.

I don't remember when I first admired Dan's colorful impressionist paintings on the walls of our mutual friends' homes. Apparently, he took up painting in the early eighties, when his daughter Lauren discovered some pen and ink drawings he had done while at NYU and encouraged him. In any event, he was exhibiting his work regularly by 2009 when Andy and I were invited to a "sip and see" featuring the Bervs' first grandchild, Penny, born to their daughter, Lauren Berv Papadin, and her husband, Sasha. The afternoon party took place between Christmas and New Year's Eve, and since our Lauren was home from college for the holidays, I asked if she might attend with us. The Bervs graciously included her—after all, their Lauren had been one of our Lauren's favorite babysitters.

My outstanding memory from that day, other than the adorable baby, is observing my daughter engrossed in conversation with Dan about his art, which surrounded us in his and Barbara's Hilltop home. There was chemistry between them—in Dan's words—"a sharing of positive energy". We drove the few blocks back to our house afterward with Lauren excitedly telling us Dan had invited her to visit his studio. After graduating from Dartmouth in June and returning to Denver, she took him up on his invitation, and in 2011 purchased one of his paintings, a small canvas I am sure Dan discounted heavily for her because she loved it so much. Lauren had become a follower, attending as many of Dan's shows as she could, sometimes running into Alex, who faithfully assisted his father in setting up and taking down his exhibits. Once, at the Cheesman Park Art Fest, a large, juried show held annually in Denver, a late afternoon storm erupted as Lauren strolled among the tents, and she ran to help Dan and Alex cover Dan's paintings and carry them to safety.

Dan's brother, Elliott, and his wife, Vera, divorced in 2001. Their middle son, Jason, had moved to Boulder to work on a PhD in education at the University of Colorado. There he met his wife, Sumaya Abu-Haidar, and in 2004 they founded the Watershed School, an independent non-profit middle and high school on whose Board of Trustees he still serves. In 2002, after Elliott and Vera's youngest son Peter had also moved to Colorado, staying a week in Dan and Barbara's basement and playing his didgeridoo, Jason persuaded his mother to move from Maine to be near him and Sumaya, and, in his words, "get to know your grandchildren". Today Jason and Sumaya live with sons Owen, born September 2, 2001, and Spencer, born November 15, 2003, on a ranch in Crested Butte, where they have a thriving life coach practice.

Vera, who has remained in Boulder, was delighted to renew her relationship with Dan, her former brother-in-law, in nearby Denver, with whom she and Elliott had lost touch over the years, and to have him know her sons, his nephews. Vera had been two years ahead of Dan at Great Neck South High, where they both served in student government—Dan as president of his sophomore class. During her senior year Vera often offered Dan a ride to school.

Peter, a licensed massage therapist and wellness guru, now lives near his mother in Arvada. He and his wife, Kindra Greentree, have a son, Pax, born October 31, 2019. Stella's second cousin provides her with many greatly appreciated hand-me-downs. Peter's daughter by his first marriage, Tara, born May 4, 2008, is a high school freshman, a lovely girl and a wonderful big sister.

Elliott and Vera's oldest son, David, is a chiropractic sports physician. After suffering a series of career-altering spine issues and being diagnosed in 2013 with multiple sclerosis, he founded The Float Zone—where he is Chief Experience Officer—as an alternative to surgery and pain medication, for himself and others. He and his wife of almost thirty years, Stephanie French, live in Richmond, Virginia.

Vera is still beautiful—an artist, a passionate Argentine tango dancer, and an accomplished pianist, one of the things that originally attracted Elliott to her. She has an exceptionally strong bond with her youngest son, Peter, due to his having been born with a birth condition requiring numerous surgeries and physical therapies, with Vera always at his side. Vera, Peter, and his family are regulars at Barbara and Dan's family holiday gatherings, where at Christmas Vera accompanies the singing of carols.

When I encounter Dan socially, at our traditional City Park Jazz evenings, for example, he often seems quiet and reserved. But when I sit down next to him and we begin a conversation, whether the topic is music, art, gardening, justice and equity issues, or family—especially family—he engages with passion. Dan Berv is a passionate person. Never was this more clearly demonstrated than in the spring of 2022, when Damion's wife, Denise, after suffering months of bewildering symptoms, was diagnosed with Creutzfeldt-Jakob disease, a degenerative brain disorder that brings on dementia, and ultimately, death.

Damion was distraught, of course, caring for his wife and their young son, Danny, while trying to work. Dan stepped in to help cut through the red tape preventing them from accessing assistance, and worked to get Denise into hospice, providing comfort for her and respite for Damion. Sadly, Denise passed away on June 9, 2022.

It is Dan's passion for all things good, and against all ill, that I know Stella will experience, appreciate, love, and remember about her "Pops".

Photos

The Berv Brothers

Arthur and Suzanne, Elliott and Dan

Pearl and Samuel Berv

Barbara and Leo Goldberg

Dan and Barbara w/ his Goldberg
Grandparents

Barbara Goldberg and Lavalle

Dan and Barbara

Dan and Damion

Dan's nephews - Peter, David, and
Jason, w/Vera Berv

Peter and Kindra, Tara, and Pax

Jason and Sumaya, Owen and Spencer

Fathers' Day 2020, Dan w/Stella

Damion Alexander Berv

Uncle Damion

I MET WITH DAMION on the four-month anniversary of his wife Denise's death, and he was "doing okay", he said. Soon-to-be-ten-year-old Danny popped onto the Zoom screen for a minute to say "hi", and he was as bright, both facially and verbally, as ever, though Damion told me later Danny had been emotionally overwhelmed a day earlier when they happened to drive past the hospital where Denise had stayed prior to her transfer to Denver Hospice, where she died on June 9, 2022 from Creutzfeldt-Jakob disease, at the age of fifty-three.

Damion and Denise were soulmates. She was his second wife, and he had actually met her three decades prior to their marriage, when she was dating a member of Legion of Death—LOD for short—a band Damion, whose stage name is Damion Alexander, formed in 1985 with Jeff Harmsen, Dennis Torres, and John "Death" Gottschalk. Denise dated John, who was the singer in the band, but she often hung out with Jeff and Damion. Damion said they were like the "Three Musketeers", sharing a quirky, sarcastic sense of humor. The band split up in 1989, though reorganized in 2011 with largely different members, and Damion and Denise lost track of each other. On October 22,

2010, when Damion—having moved to Portland, married, and then divorced—returned to Denver for a reunion of Bone Circus, another band he had formed almost twenty years earlier, Denise was in the audience at Bangles Nightclub in Glendale. The two talked for hours after the show, and they fell in love.

Damion Alexander Berv was born on May 22, 1968, to Daniel Alexander Berv and Faune Yerby, who had met as students at New York University. Both children of famous fathers, chances are they were attracted to each other because of their creative passions—his, music and art, and hers, poetry—but their marriage ended a little over two years after their move in 1971 from New York to Denver. When Dan met and began dating Barbara Beard in the summer of 1974, Damion was a polite and well-behaved six-year-old, and Barbara, judging Dan to have excellent parenting skills, fell in love with them both. After Dan and Barbara married in September of 1975, Damion spent increasingly more, and soon all, of his time in their home. Barbara is "Mom" to Damion, the mother he claims today.

Damion was cared for often by Carolyn, Barbara's sister, and by Gertrude, Barbara's mother. He describes his grandmother as one of the sweetest, most loving persons he ever knew. She traditionally made him a cinnamon chocolate cake for his birthday, which, as he described it to me, sounded like what I grew up calling a Texas Sheet Cake. I intend to try making it for him next May. Damion also told me about the times he visited his great-grandparents, Leo and Barbara Goldberg, in Palm Springs. As he grew older, he sometimes stayed alone with them, his parents checking in at a hotel nearby, and as an older teen he flew out to visit alone, once with his best friend. He couldn't get over the novelty of being in a swimming pool in December when the family once visited at Christmas. As have all the Bervs, Damion told me about Lavalle, his great-grandparents' companion and caregiver, "an angel in human form, and the best cook ever". He remembers Lavalle's huge salads, wonderful steaks, and unbelievable homemade German chocolate cakes.

Damion got seriously into music around the age of ten. When he was five, he accompanied his father in Dan's Volkswagen bug on a trip to California to visit friends in San Francisco. Father and son went to a park where a group of musicians were jamming. Dan introduced himself and took over the Congas, convincing Damion on the spot that he was the coolest dad in the world. When Damion learned to play, it was on Dan's drums—the same set he had been playing the night he met Barbara. This love of music has been a natural bond between Damion and Dan, even as their preferred genres diverged, with Damion progressing from heavy metal to thrash, maximizing on his love of percussion.

Damion was very fond of his younger siblings, but he and Alex, with whom he liked to roughhouse and wrestle, were especially close. When Damion moved into his own condominium, which featured a fish tank, and a waterbed flanked by matching speakers, Alex would often spend the night. On those occasions they ordered the Pudge Brothers Pudgy B pizza—a meat lovers' pie with pepperoni, hamburger, Italian sausage, and Canadian bacon—and watched the Nuggets or the Grizzlies, a minor league hockey team which enjoyed a brief stint in Denver. The condo belonged to Dan, who upon Damion's high school graduation offered him the choice of living at home for $300 per month in rent or living in the condominium—which Dan had purchased as an investment—for $350 per month. It was not a difficult decision to make.

Damion's preferred sport has always been basketball; as a teen he and Alex spent hours shooting baskets together in the back driveway of the Bervs' home in Hilltop. Today Damion shoots baskets with Danny, the son born to him and Denise on January 18, 2013. At

almost ten years Danny has high ambitions—to play for the NBA—
and according to Damion, his son is good.

As a young adult Damion babysat for both Lauren and Alex. He
suspects that Lauren, ten years younger and "preppy", was a little
embarrassed by her long-haired brother and his heavy metal friends.
"She was so smart", he told me, "and she had a million friends."

Damion, whose idols included Van Halen and Kiss, could probably have made a living as a musician. LOD had numerous engagements in Denver—on its own and opening for other major record
label bands. In 1988 *Denver Westword* magazine named LOD "Best
Underground Band". But as important to him as music has always
been and continues to be, Damion's professional career has been in
the insurance industry—primarily health insurance, including disability and long-term care—working in finance and administration
for large employers like BlueCross BlueShield of Colorado, and the
Regence Group, an affiliation of BlueCross and BlueShield plans in the
Pacific Northwest/Mountain region.

Damion's employer at the time of this writing is Assure
Neuromonitoring. This publicly traded Denver-based company provides highly trained technicians and interpreting physicians to assist
surgeons, by monitoring a variety of surgeries in real time. This service, known as inter-operative neuromonitoring, or IONM, is demonstrated to improve patient outcomes, but is often considered medically
unnecessary by insurance companies. Damion, with his extensive
background in insurance contract interpretation and claims administration, formerly wrote appeals on behalf of patients to their insurance
companies, advocating for payment for IONM. Today, however, he
works in revenue cycle management for the company.

Damion and his first wife, Cyndi Hackett, worked for the same
insurance company in the early nineties. They began dating, then
decided to take a vacation together. They randomly chose Portland,

Oregon as their destination. They liked it so much that, back in Denver, Damion subscribed to the *Oregonian* newspaper, checking the employment ads regularly. In 1993 he landed a job in Portland, and he and Cyndi moved there together. Several years later, they were married in a ceremony on Bandon Beach. The Oregon lifestyle suited them and their Keeshond dogs, and they enjoyed making new friends and building bonfires on the beach. Cyndi was a little "kookie", according to Damion's cousin, Jeanna. She had a warm personality, and an interest in the metaphysical.

During Damion's time in Portland Alex flew out to visit him numerous times. He would always arrive carrying his basketball, and the two of them would pick up where they had left off in Denver. In May of 2008, twenty-five-year-old Alex flew to Portland to help Damion celebrate his fortieth birthday, together with a big group of friends, on the beach. The weather was unseasonably hot, over a hundred degrees, and Damion dived into the ocean wearing a brand new, and very expensive, pair of sunglasses which he promptly lost in the crashing waves—his birthday offering to the ocean gods.

Damion lived in Portland for twenty years, during which time he and Cyndi divorced, and he might never have left were it not for the chance reunion with Denise. His best friends are the ones he met there, and they stay in close touch. But Denise was in Denver. She had a son, Zach Bakko, from her previous marriage, and she was not interested in moving. So, Damion came home to Denver, to marry Denise, and to welcome Danny into their lives on January 18, 2013. Denise was a wonderful mother, Damion told me, a "bright light".

Now, with Denise's passing, Damion wonders what the future may bring. He has his music, and he hopes to pursue another interest of his, photography, in a more intentional way. He is devoted to Danny, and his extended family is devoted to them both. Damion is a man of faith, and is convinced that whatever happens next, God is with him. Amen.

Photos

Damion, around age twelve

Damion with his mother
and sister, with Lavalle

Damion and his siblings

Damion and his family on
Bandon Beach

Damion Alexander, around forty

Damion's wife Denise, on their wedding day

Denise and Danny

Damion and Danny

Lauren Michelle Berv Papadin

Aunt Lauren

LAUREN PAPADIN IS A force of nature—educator, world traveler, and mother—whom I first met when she came to our Cherry Creek condominium in September of 1993 at age fourteen to babysit. She was precocious, polite, and totally engaged with six-year-old Lauren Kenney, her charge for the evening. At that time she was a freshman at Manual High School, where she graduated in 1997, having attended Hill Middle School and Carson Elementary. Lauren's years at Manual were the final four in a twenty-year integration plan mandated for Denver Public Schools with the goal of creating a diverse socio-economic student body. Lauren describes this "sanction" as a gift and wishes it had not ended. She loved each of the public schools she attended and makes it a point to walk past them when in Denver.

Lauren Michelle Berv was born on December 17, 1978, to parents Dan (Pops) and Barbara (Momma). She grew up the only daughter and a middle child—brothers Damion and Alex were ten years older and four years younger, respectively. She felt valued and loved by her parents, and free to be herself.

When visiting colleges her senior year of high school Lauren fell in love with California, specifically with the San Francisco Bay Area, and made Santa Clara, a prestigious Jesuit liberal arts school, her first choice. She loved all genres of literature, so chose English as her major, but after a junior year abroad in San Sebastian, Spain, changed to Modern Foreign Languages, with Spanish as her focus. After graduation from Santa Clara in 2001, Lauren traveled in South America for a year, living first in Santiago, Chile, where she taught English, then moving south to a beautiful village situated at the foot of a volcano called Pucon, in the southern lake district of Chile. These immersion experiences firmly established Spanish as her second language, a language she continues to speak with fluency.

After this post-graduate year abroad, Lauren returned to Denver for two years. She worked as a group living counselor at a residential and day treatment center for girls, one of the most difficult but meaningful jobs she ever held. Working with eleven-to-thirteen-year-olds with extreme behaviors and compelling stories, she learned to balance compassion, boundaries, and tough love.

In 2004, Lauren attended a friend's wedding in San Francisco, and realized she had to move back to the Bay Area, which she did in late summer of that year. She found a job running the children's program for an agency that assisted families experiencing homelessness. Working with these children, and with their mothers, she learned a lot about the intersecting cycles of poverty and homelessness.

Just a few months after settling into life in San Francisco, a friend introduced Lauren to Sasha Papadin, her husband-to-be. Lauren describes their attraction as "love at second sight", as "it was the moment he came back to my house a few weeks later that I lost my breath when finding him at my doorstep." Sasha soon took Lauren up to Sonoma to meet his family—his father, Val, his mother, Nella, and his six siblings. After playing the piano for her at the farmhouse he was living in, Sasha took Lauren to dinner at Val's home. His parents were divorced but on friendly terms, and Nella came around that night with Sasha's sister, Natasha. The next day they all had tea at Nella's home. By the end of the weekend Lauren was sure she wanted to marry Sasha, and to become a part of this fascinating and very special family.

Sasha's parents met when Nella, who was English, traveled to St. Petersburg, Russia's cultural center, in her early twenties. There she was introduced into a group of artistic young people that included a dissident poet named Valentin Papadin, with whom she fell in love. Val had feigned madness to escape military service, and was on a KGB (Komitet Gosudarstvennoy Bezopasnosti, or "Committee for State Security", in English) watch list at the time, but the couple boldly and successfully made plans for him to return to England with Nella, most likely with the assistance of an insider who knew how to get him out of the Soviet Union. The two married, and their first child, Sasha, was born on September 26, 1980.

England was not home to Val, so the couple tried making a new life in Italy, where they taught English, but this was not home either. They decided to come to the United States, where in the winter of 1986 they arrived at the Holy Virgin Catholic Church, a Russian Orthodox church located on Geary Street in the Richmond District of San Francisco. Soon after, when Sasha was eight years old, they welcomed his baby sister, Natasha, followed in rapid succession by Susie, William, Anastasia, Gregory, and Henry. It is said that the oldest child often becomes the third parent, and in Sasha's case this was especially true, given the age difference between him and his closest sibling. Sasha had an older half-brother Yuri - Val's son by his first marriage to a Russian woman - who in 1993 joined the family in California. It was Yuri who officiated the marriage between Lauren and Sasha on October 13, 2007, in Sonoma, surrounded by their loved ones.

Lauren moved to Sonoma in 2005, one year after meeting Sasha, leaving her job in San Francisco and going to work as a learning specialist at an independent school in Marin County. On June 30, 2009, she gave birth to Penny. Teddy was born on December 13, 2011.

In 2014 she reconnected with a professional colleague with whom she had worked in Marin, and the two of them contracted for office space together. After sharing an office for three years, they formalized their partnership and founded Spark Whole Student Learning, offering tutoring services for students from kindergarten to twelfth grade, "with a special focus on building confidence, executive functioning, and self-advocacy skills". While Lauren has always loved working with children, most of her time these days is spent working with parents, tutors, teachers and specialists in support of each unique student. Her sister-in-law Natasha is now Spark's Director of Operations.

Reflecting on her own childhood, Lauren remembers her mother as warm, fun, and loving whilst magically juggling the demands of work responsibilities and family time. When Barbara needed help with childcare she often turned to her older sister, Carolyn, and to her mother, Gertrude, and Lauren loved spending time with both. Carolyn took Lauren, who enjoyed being her "sidekick", along with her when running errands. Grandma Gertrude was warm and kind, and lots of fun. She made delicious crepes, filled with jam and sprinkled with powdered sugar, and she always seemed to know how to make a sick grandchild feel better. Lauren remembers seeing her grandmother upset only once, and that was when she and Alex were being rambunctious and indulging in sibling rivalry.

Gertrude was the only grandparent Lauren knew, though for a time she corresponded with Suzanne Berv, her father's mother. She has fond memories of visiting her great-grandmother, Barbara Goldberg, in Palm Springs—of the pool, the grapefruit trees, dancing for her in the evenings, and the big bear hugs from Lavalle, the Goldbergs' devoted carer. She especially loved seeing her dad's pure joy and the deep love he felt for his grandparents, and how happy he was to share that with his own family.

One of the things that attracted Lauren and Sasha to each other is their love of music. A professional woodworker and furniture maker by trade, Sasha owns Pinocchio Furniture in Sonoma. He is also a professional musician who loves to collaborate. His first band, The Val Papadins, released an album titled *No One Wants to Move the Piano* in 2007, and in recent years he has performed solo as Loverman. Lauren played piano in one of his previous bands but prefers to be in the crowd, in her words "crooning and swaying".

Lauren herself does not know how she came by her adventuresome spirit. As a girl she loved going to sleepovers and overnight camps. She insisted on going away to college, and her love of travel is legend in the family. But none of the Bervs was prepared for her announcement in the spring of 2021 that she and Sasha and their children would be moving to Bath, England in the fall. They would live with one of Nella's surviving sisters, Marina (tragically, Nella died in 2020 after a battle with breast cancer), and Penny and Teddy would attend King Edward's School for the 2021-22 term. The first year went so well that the family of four moved into their own rented flat and extended their stay for a second year. Fortunately, Lauren's parents were able to visit her and her family in April of 2022 and will visit again in November. Lauren brought the children to visit Baba and Pops in Denver during the summer between their visits to England.

Lauren and Sasha have been able to maintain their businesses while living abroad, and Sasha is now writing, recording, and preparing for a small United Kingdom tour with a group of musicians who are, as he, Californians living in the UK. Lauren describes this two-year stay as a particularly fun way to travel as a family, immersing themselves in the culture and getting to know the people. She loves the surroundings, the Roman architecture of Bath, and its abounding natural beauty and open space. Sasha and Lauren have family and friends nearby, in Brighton, Bristol, and the Cotswolds, and in Italy, Spain, and Greece, so the children continue to be reared by a village.

Penny and Teddy love their English school, where the academics and extracurriculars are excellent. For now, Penny is totally committed to her musical theatre training, which focuses on integrating acting, singing, and dance. She is writing her own music, and is often observed practicing choreography or memorizing the lines for her next play. In December of 2022 she will take the Trinity Musical Theatre Exam, a certificate program sponsored by Trinity College, London.

Teddy has excelled at sports since he was a toddler; for years I have heard what a gifted athlete he is. Currently he is playing rugby and running cross country at King Edward's. Outside of school hours he is being coached in tennis development, his latest passion. Lauren shared a sweet story with me about her son. When Penny was still a toddler, Lauren became pregnant again, but miscarried. I remember this event, because Barbara, her mother, canceled a trip to Santa Fe with our birthday group at the last minute to be with her daughter in California. When Lauren became pregnant a third time, and she and Sasha went for an ultrasound, the image of their male baby signaled to them from the womb—with a thumbs up—that everything would be fine. As a child, Teddy was slow to verbalize, but he often reassured his parents with a thumbs up.

The Papadins enjoyed a wonderful visit to the United States in the summer of 2022, cherishing their time with family and other loved ones. They feel a pull between the two worlds of the UK and the US. While Sonoma's extreme weather events related to climate change—drought and wildfires—are difficult to navigate, they love their community there, aunties and uncles dotting the coastline, their friends who have become like family and are considered unofficial godparents, and the year-round abundance of fresh ingredients for their big family meals.

California and Colorado are not that far apart, the world is small, and cousins are special. Penny, Teddy, Danny, and Stella will continue to make many fun memories together over the years to come.

Photos

Lauren at two years

Lauren's Manual High School senior pic

Lauren and her family of birth

Lauren and Sasha, with her parents, Damion and Cyndi, and Alex

Lauren and Sasha and family

Penny Papadin

Teddy Papadin

Penny and Teddy

Alex Richard Berv

Daddy

ALEX WAS BORN SEPTEMBER 4, 1982, at Saint Joseph Hospital in Denver. Though his sister Lauren's delivery had lasted eighteen hours, their mother, Barbara, told me that Alex entered the world "easily, and kind." This kindness is one of Alex's most endearing traits, and one that—according to his father, Dan, speaking recently on the occasion of Alex's fortieth birthday—just gets better with age. I have heard my husband, Andy, say to friends and members of *our* family that our son-in-law is the nicest person he has ever met.

When Alex was born, the Berv family lived at 714 Ivanhoe Street. One of Alex's earliest memories takes place in this home. He is sitting in his crib, feeling cozy and secure, just staring at the wallpaper. Alex's sister, Lauren, is four years older than he, and half-brother Damion fourteen years older, so each child had his own room—Damion's in the basement, where teenagers often prefer to be. When Alex was almost three the family moved from the Mayfair neighborhood to a much larger home in Hilltop. Alex, wearing his superhero cape, would run back and forth across the main level of the house, from the dining room at one end to the living room at the opposite, and he and Lauren enjoyed shouting into the seemingly cavernous rooms to hear their voices echo prior to the time Barbara was able to get rugs down and carpet installed.

As a toddler, Alex was cared for by a woman named Dura, who had a young child of her own, but when he turned four, he entered Cherry Creek Preschool, located at Fourth Avenue and Columbine Street, in the neighborhood known as Cherry Creek North. Here Alex met his new best friend, David Shams, with whom he remained close for most of his childhood.

Alex and David became immersed in the culture of Teenage Mutant Ninja Turtles, all the rage for young boys (and girls) at the time. These fictional humanoids were supposedly formed when four baby turtles were released into the sewer system of New York City and exposed to radioactive waste. They became crime fighters, super-heroes named after famous Italian artists, each with a distinct personality. David's favorite turtle was Michaelangelo, the most fun-loving of the four, who wore an orange bandana and loved pepperoni pizza. Alex's was Raphael, the strongest and most reckless. His bandana was red, and he sported a pair of sai, a Japanese weapon that looks like a hairpin. The other two turtles were Leonardo and Donatello. In 1990 the turtles went on a national concert tour sponsored by Pizza Hut, performing songs such as *Coming Out of Our Shells*, and *Cowabunga*. Alex and David attended this concert at the Denver Coliseum in November of that year.

Initially Alex attended the neighborhood schools to which he was assigned, Carson Elementary and Hill Middle School. When the time came for high school, however, his sister insisted he apply to attend East—the oldest high school in Denver, located in a beautiful historic building across the street from City Park—rather than George Washington, located nearer the family's home. This turned out to be good counsel.

Barbara worked while her children were growing up, and as did I, she took advantage of the many excellent enrichment programs and sports camps available to our children when school was not in session. Around the age of four or five, Alex attended a summer day-camp at the Jewish Community Center and was somehow left outside the building when the children returned from a field trip. When Barbara came to pick him up at the end of the day, he was standing in front of the JCC, swinging his backpack and clearly in a pique. He had waited there for well over an hour, alone. Getting into the car he calmly told his mother, "I'm just a little bit mad at you." Barbara, when she learned what had happened, was furious.

Alex's kindness and his even temperament—to one who does not know him well—might belie his determination. Alex is the first person you want on your side if there is a problem with an airline, hotel, or restaurant reservation, or any other situation in which your expectations have not been met (unless the situation involves plumbing, in which case you want his wife and my daughter, Lauren). Alex is clear-headed—not overly reactive, but thoughtfully responsive. These qualities have contributed to his success in business and in life.

Alex likes baseball, but he loves basketball, and always has. But at five feet, eight inches tall, playing on a team—especially at a competitive school like East—was not an option beyond the freshman squad. So, he shot baskets with his brother and his friends at the hoop his father installed in the driveway of their home, and supported Denver's professional team, the Nuggets.

In addition to influencing Alex's high school choice, his sister counseled him on what to wear, what classes to take, and who to make friends with. Lauren herself had attended Manual High, but the school had fallen on challenging times after 1995, when the district ended the busing it had implemented to achieve integration. Lauren encouraged Alex to develop a diverse group of friends, which he did, several of which—including his best friend John Bitzanakis—he remains close to today.

Alex's favorite classes (after Physical Education) were those that allowed him to express his creativity—especially by writing. He is a good writer, and writing is an important part of his work today. Alex's psychology teacher, Mr. Hernandez, nominated him to travel to Israel as part of an America-Israel Friendship League program designed to strengthen ties between the two countries. After a rigorous application process, which no doubt involved a writing sample, Alex was chosen for the three-week trip, and in the fall of his junior year traveled to three Israeli cities—Tel Aviv, Jerusalem, and Haifa—speaking to, and meeting with, other high school students. The stated purpose of this cultural exchange program was a focus on the two countries' shared democratic values. But Alex was surprised to discover the many other things he had in common with these students, including the music they listened to, and the sports they participated in. He describes this experience (which, as an aside, included kissing two different girls in one day) as life changing.

After high school graduation Alex attended the University of Colorado Leeds School of Business, where he was a member of the interdisciplinary Presidents Leadership Class, a scholar community emphasizing leadership development through curriculum and experience. A focus on understanding key social issues led early on to his enrollment in a class on diversity and inclusion at the university's Denver campus one summer. This was among the best courses he took while at CU. It enhanced his continuously growing interest in and acceptance of people from various backgrounds. It also served to make him more aware of his own privilege, and contributed to his desire to help lift others up, especially disadvantaged youth. Alex has been a generous supporter of organizations such as Urban Peak and the Denver Public Schools Foundation.

Alex lived on campus during his freshman year, but afterward lived in a series of Boulder apartments with a variety of roommates. The second semester of his junior year he co-authored a textbook entitled *Profiles in Business and Society*. This was the basis for a course he taught during his senior year. In June of 2005, Alex received a Bachelor of Science degree in business, with a double-major in marketing and management.

After graduating from CU Alex went to work for Integro, a Denver-based software company founded by computer executive and entrepreneur Scott Burt. The company had been named by *Inc.* magazine as "one of the 500 fastest growing companies in America" in early 2000, only to be shot down by the dotcom bust later that same year, when three of the company's largest four clients retreated. Burt had cut his staff of sixty down to seventeen by 2002 but was beginning to rebuild by the time Alex graduated and joined the firm.

Alex's sales success at Integro, where he worked his way into the position of Business Development Manager, allowed him to purchase his first home, a two-bedroom condominium located on St. Paul Street, just south of City Park, on the redeveloped site of the former Provenant Mercy Hospital. Alex is disciplined in his financial affairs, and by the time of his marriage to Lauren in 2017, his mortgage had almost been paid in full.

When Integro was acquired by Innovative Discovery in 2020, around the time of Alex's fifteen- year anniversary with the company, he was somewhat concerned to now be working for a company headquartered in Virginia. But he need not have been, as his abilities to communicate with prospective clients and patiently guide them through the sales process continued to be highly valued by ID. No doubt Alex's loyalty to his employers—the same loyalty he demonstrates in his relationships with friends and family—has contributed to his business success. The product Alex sells to Fortune 100 companies is essentially software that allows them to rid themselves of data they continue to store, but no longer use. Alex has said to me on more than one occasion "If Hillary Clinton had only been using our product…" referring to the private server scandal that plagued the Democratic presidential candidate in 2016.

Growing up, Alex was close to his maternal grandmother, and it was clear she adored him. The family chuckles about the time his sister returned from a year spent in Chile after college graduation and went to visit Gertrude. "Did you miss me, Grandma?" Lauren asked, upon entering their grandmother's apartment, to which Gertrude, who was now suffering from dementia, responded, "Where's Alex?" Barbara's mother was the only grandparent Alex knew. However, he was also close to his great-grandmother, Barbara Goldberg, his father's maternal grandmother, who called Alex her "Gold-mensch" perhaps loosely translated as her treasure or her angel. The Bervs traveled regularly to Palm Springs to visit Grandma Barb. Her late husband, Leo, or Gramps had died in 1980, two years before Alex was born. Alex has fond memories of these family vacations, of playing in the pool with his sister and looking up at the palm trees, which he claims today as his favorite kind of tree. He also remembers the wonderful Lavalle.

In addition to flawlessly clear skin and beautiful eyes (a genetic anomaly has given him two rows of upper eyelashes rather than one—a trait most women would kill for), Alex has an imposing physique, honed since graduation from CU when he decided to shed, as he describes it, more than the "freshman fifteen", referring to the extra poundage college students often add when they leave their mother's healthy home cooking for dorm food. Since his father was a runner, he decided to try that, and ran a half-marathon with his sister before running a full marathon in 2010. At age forty he no longer runs as often, but works out in his home gym or at his club gym faithfully.

He credits this habit as the source of not only his physical but his mental health.

When I asked Alex for his worst memory, he did not hesitate to admit that he was forced to spend a night in jail, and not just any night, but the night of his eighteenth birthday. Having gone out late in the evening with friends for Taco Bell (which coincidentally was always my Lauren's late-night craving), he was pulled over by the police on what turned out to be a mistaken arrest warrant. However, because he had encountered the law on two previous occasions for smoking marijuana, he was taken into custody. To make matters worse, he was wearing shorts, but no shoes or shirt. The items of clothing provided him downtown did not, as he put it, "help his street cred".

These incidents were an anomaly. Alex was always the "good boy", the child who never talked back to his parents, who did whatever they asked of him. He maintained good grades, was respected by his teachers, and was empathetic to a diverse group of friends. He complained to me that it was so unfair that he had to spend a night in jail—that his siblings did far worse and never got caught. I kidded him by suggesting that perhaps he was just not very good at being bad. I have since learned that the Bervs tease Alex often about being a "bad" criminal. Thankfully, the arrests were erased from the record.

Alex has always been close to his sister, but he was also close to Damion, despite the fourteen- year difference in their ages. As a little boy he wrestled with his older brother. He always felt his older brother's love and respect, and when Damion, as a young adult, moved to Portland, Oregon, Alex visited on multiple occasions. There they went on sight-seeing expeditions, shopping for CDs, and drums. Alex describes Damion as very parental toward him on these occasions.

Alex is fun to travel with. He is nonplussed when faced with driving in a new area; now Andy and I know to put Alex's name on the rental car contract so that we can just sit in the back seat and relax.

He always seems to find the best restaurants and hotels. And he is fun to hang out with, always up for a new experience, like learning pickleball on a recent trip to Austin for my cousin Tina's sixty-fifth birthday bash. This same trip he managed to stay calm and composed over a three-night stay in a six-bedroom vacation rental with seven Hester relatives.

On another trip, to Hawaii, Alex agreed to let Andy, Lauren, and me teach him to play bridge. We started out teaching him to play spades, at which he became proficient. We then explained that bridge is like spades, but that any card suit could now be "trump". On the first hand dealt, it was three passes to Alex, an indication he probably held most of the face cards (either that, or they were evenly distributed among us). His eyes were big, as he said, "I don't even know what to do with this hand." "How many points do you have?", Lauren asked. "Twenty-six", he said. I said, "Then you should open two clubs." Andy said, "It doesn't have anything to do with clubs. Lauren (Alex's partner) will say two diamonds, nothing to do with diamonds. Then you can bid your hand." Alex exclaimed in frustration, "I feel like you guys are speaking Japanese!" It was hilarious.

One characteristic I feel defines Alex, and that attracted our daughter to him early on, is his love for his family—for his parents, siblings, and cousins—and his desire to be close to them and spend time with them. Though Lauren and Alex like to travel, especially to California, Hawaii, and Mexico, where they enjoy not only the palm trees but the umbrella drinks, they do not see themselves living anywhere but Denver. This comforts me, and gives me confidence we may grow old with our children around us, blessed to enjoy each new stage of Stella's life.

Photos

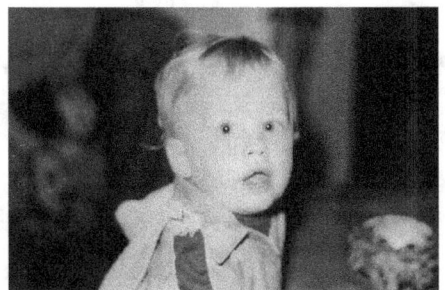

Super-hero Alex

Alex with Damion

Alex in space

On the baseball field

Alex's East High School senior pic

Marathon run with his sister, Lauren

Sweet Grandma Gertrude

Alex and groomsmen Peter, John, Lucien, Bradon, and Damion

Alex and his siblings

Alex and his parents

Alex, Lauren, and Stella in Hawaii

Part Two

The Stitching

How it Happened

ALEX AND LAUREN BEGAN their courtship on June 21, 2014. It was shamelessly promoted by their mothers, but it took a little time.

As reported earlier, the Kenneys attended a "sip and see" for six-month-old Penny Papadin at the Bervs' home the week after Christmas in 2009. There our Lauren reconnected with their Lauren, who had been a favorite babysitter years earlier. The Papadins lived in Sonoma and were in Denver for the holidays. The Bervs' younger son, Alex, was also at the party. This is the first time Andy and I met our future son-in-law, but he and our daughter did not seem to notice each other that day. Instead, our Lauren was deeply engrossed in conversation with Dan Berv on a topic they are both passionate about—art. She was taking a course in abstract expressionism at the time, which is Dan's dominant style of painting.

Back in Denver after graduation from Dartmouth in June of 2010, Lauren received email invitations to Dan's exhibits regularly. On November 11, 2011 she attended an event at Dan's studio and purchased a painting from him. This is the night that Lauren met Alex for the first time. After that she often saw Alex at Dan's exhibits, as he regularly helped his father set up and take down his work after a show. They were always friendly to each other.

Lauren dated several different men over the next few years. We liked them all but could not imagine our daughter married to any of them. At one point, in 2013, I suggested to Barbara that perhaps if Alex and Lauren were ever between relationships at the same time, we might try getting them together. She liked the idea, and soon invited us all to a backyard party she and Dan were giving to show off the stunning gardens he designed each summer. Lauren brought a girlfriend, Eva, and Alex was there with his friends, but the timing was still not right.

The following spring, we tried again. By now Lauren was somewhat complicit, and this time it was she who suggested inviting the Bervs over for a casual dinner the night of Monday, May 26, 2014. In writing this sequence, I realized that date was exactly one week after Andy's stroke. I have double-checked his medical records, and Lauren has shown me her paper calendar—we are both sure about these dates. It is hard to believe we did not cancel the plan. I remember it as being a lovely evening, and Andy remembers nothing, for obvious reasons. I do know that I served burgers, and was embarrassed to have Lauren tell me months later that Alex thought the main course was an appetizer. I did not yet know about his ravenous appetite, which, fortunately, is offset by his commitment to exercise.

For as long as I have known them, the Bervs have observed Sunday night City Park Jazz as a summer ritual. They always arrive early and hold a spot in front of the bandstand for a big group of family and friends. CPJ is a fun, diverse, happening scene, but one Andy and I had never gotten into. This changed in the summer of 2014, when, during the dinner at our house, Dan and Barbara suggested we join them, and offered to pick Lauren up early for the first event—Hazel Miller opening the 2014 season on the following Sunday, the first of June.

Sitting on our picnic blanket and sipping wine on three consecutive Sunday evenings, I watched Lauren and Alex talk and laugh and look into each other's eyes. I told our friend Jan Netting, Barbara's best friend from childhood, about our matchmaking attempts. She in turn told her son Matt, who agreed that Lauren and Alex were perfect for each other. This affirmation emboldened me to comment to Barbara that if Alex invited Lauren out, I was sure she would say "yes".

The invitation came quickly—for a hike in the mountains the following Saturday, the twenty-first of June. Alex offered to pack a lunch and said he would pick Lauren up at nine o'clock. She organized her gear and went to bed early Friday night, only to wake up the next morning feeling nervous that Alex might be late. He arrived at eight-fifty-nine, and Andy and I breathed a sigh of relief.

That afternoon about three o'clock, Alex brought Lauren home, and asked if he could pick her up in an hour to attend the festival held annually at the Greek Orthodox Cathedral a few blocks from our house. From the Greek Festival, they went to Second Home, a restaurant formerly located in the Cherry Creek J.W. Marriot (which is why they chose that venue for their rehearsal dinner three years later). By this time, they were so obviously smitten with each other that another couple sitting nearby asked them how long they had been married. They laughed and responded, "We've only been dating one day, but this is our third date." From that time on they only had eyes for each other.

One of the many things Lauren and Alex discovered they had in common is their love of rap and hip hop. I write earlier of Lauren's experience with open mic, but according to her, Alex's musical talent—perhaps passed down from his grandfather and his father—manifests in his ability to freestyle rap for hours, with rarely a revision.

Our family brought in the New Year, 2015, in Tucson, Arizona, one of our favorite winter vacation spots. Lauren thought about inviting Alex to join us, decided against it, then spent the entire time wishing she had. She did not make the same mistake a year later, and we had lots of fun introducing Alex to our favorite nine-hole golf course at the Hilton El Conquistador.

In June of 2016 the entire Hester family attended my nephew and godson Thomas's wedding in Austin, Texas. It was an over-the-top beautiful and fun event, and Lauren and Alex enjoyed exploring Austin together, even in the extreme heat.

Early Christmas morning that same year, Lauren texted a picture of her left hand, with the engagement ring Alex had just placed on her finger. This was on a Sunday; later they met Andy and me for worship at Central Presbyterian Church, where she continued to sparkle and glow. Later that day we continued to celebrate at the Bervs' home with their extended families.

Andy and I were set to leave Denver on the twenty-ninth of December for a two-month work-related stay in Austin, traveling through Santa Fe and Lubbock. By the time we drove away that day, we had talked to Pastor Louise Westfall, reserved the church and the organist for the wedding, and secured a venue for the reception.

On June 18, 2017, Lauren and Alex were married at Central Presbyterian Church in a beautiful and traditional four o'clock service. The reception afterward was held at the Grant-Humphreys Mansion, across a grassy knoll from the Colorado governor's residence at the Boettcher Mansion. If anything was not perfect, I would prefer not to know about it at this late date.

Over Christmas of 2019, Lauren and Alex were excitedly announcing and anticipating the expected birth of a daughter. Little did they know how much the world would change over the next five months. Stella Irene Berv was born on June 1, 2020, during a world-wide pandemic. Lauren had gone to Rose Hospital that day for a Cesarean birth, after the baby had unexpectedly changed position the day before. Barbara and Dan Berv sat with Andy and me on our back patio that evening, enjoying a cocktail together and waiting, when

Alex texted the first picture of our newborn granddaughter to our four mobile phones. A cry of joy went up, so that our next-door neighbors, the Newells, came over to the fence to congratulate us.

That joy has continued, and multiplied, as we share birthdays, holidays, and other happy occasions. Even the sad times are easier to bear together. Watching our children parent is among the most rewarding experiences we can have, and Lauren and Alex are doing it so well. Stella looks very much like the little boy her father was, except at those times when she looks almost exactly like her mother. At two years and six months her unique and precious spirit is shining through. What a gift and a blessing she is to us all.

Lauren and Alex pre-wedding

Lauren and Alex on their wedding day

Christmas 2019

Easter 2021, with Stella

Part Three

Looking Back

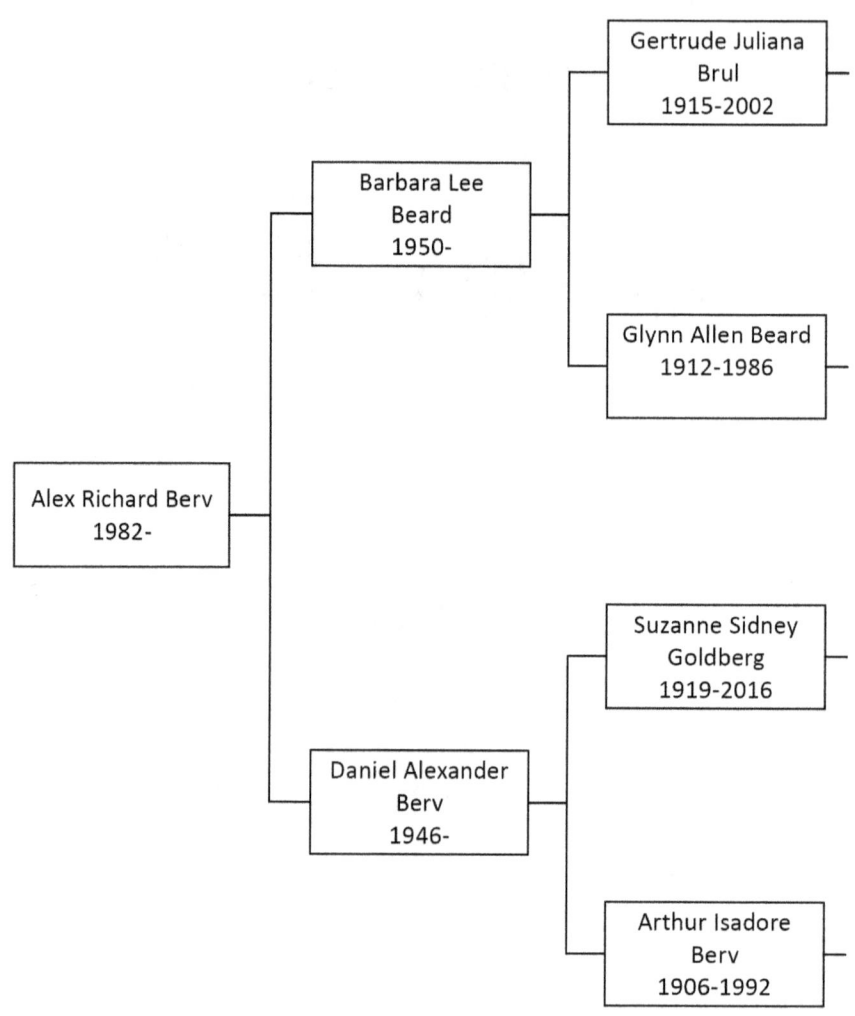

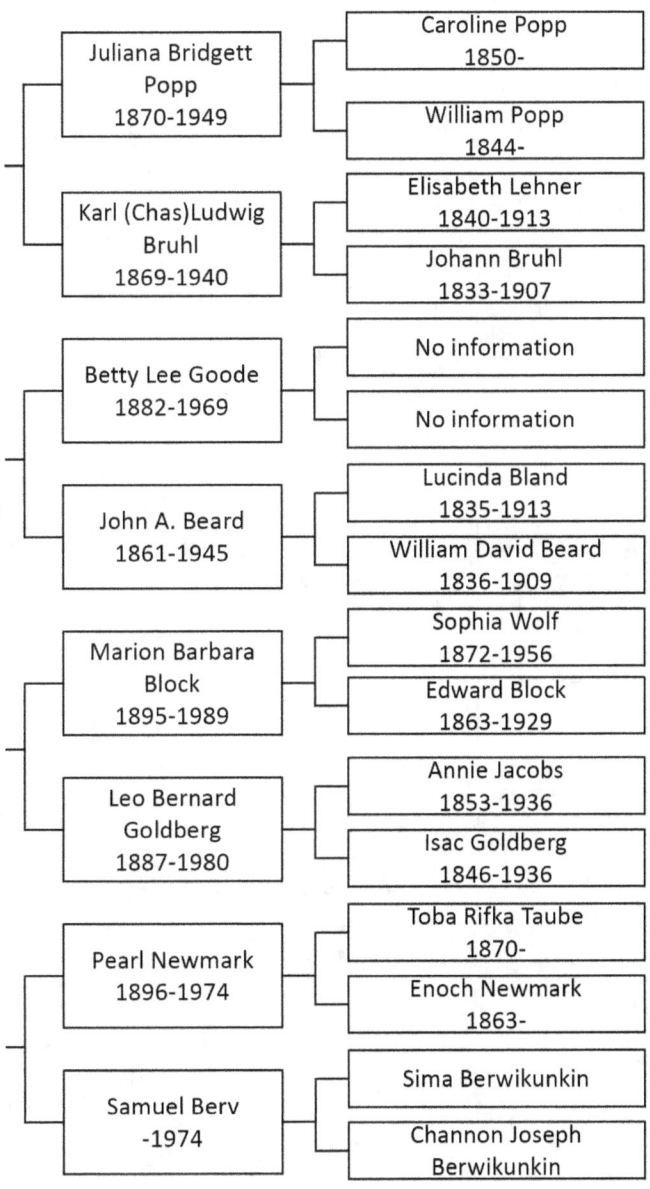

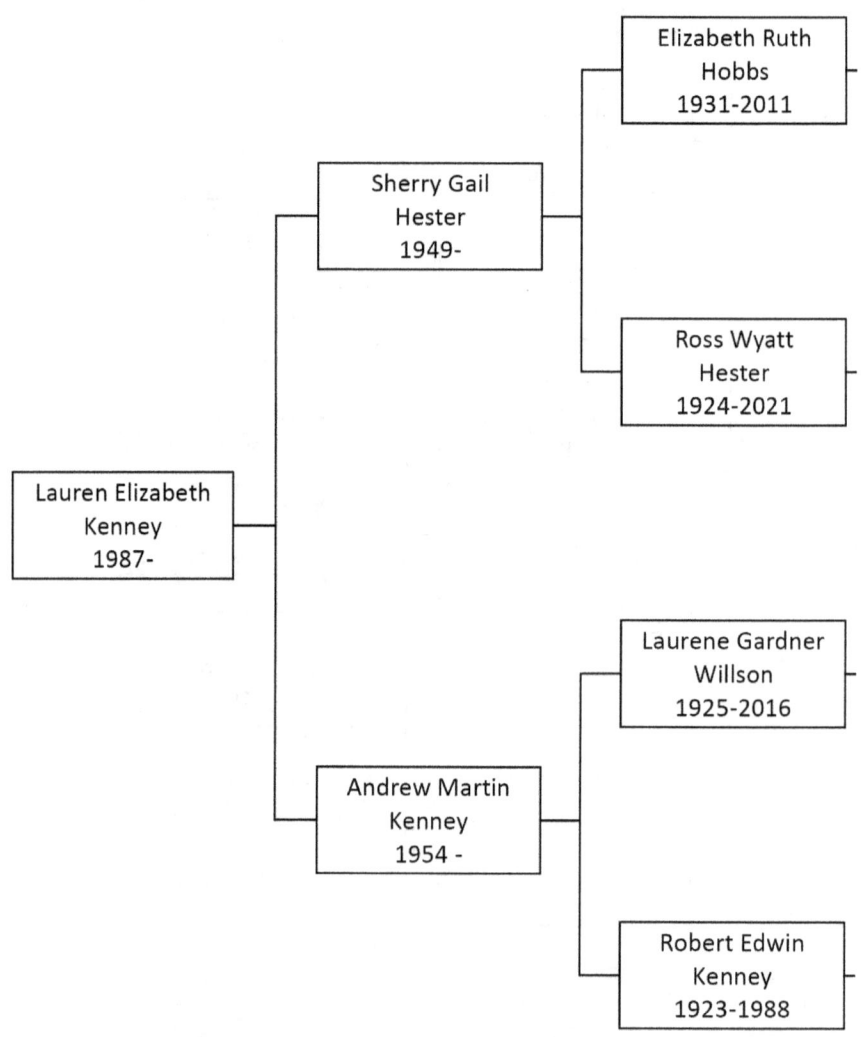

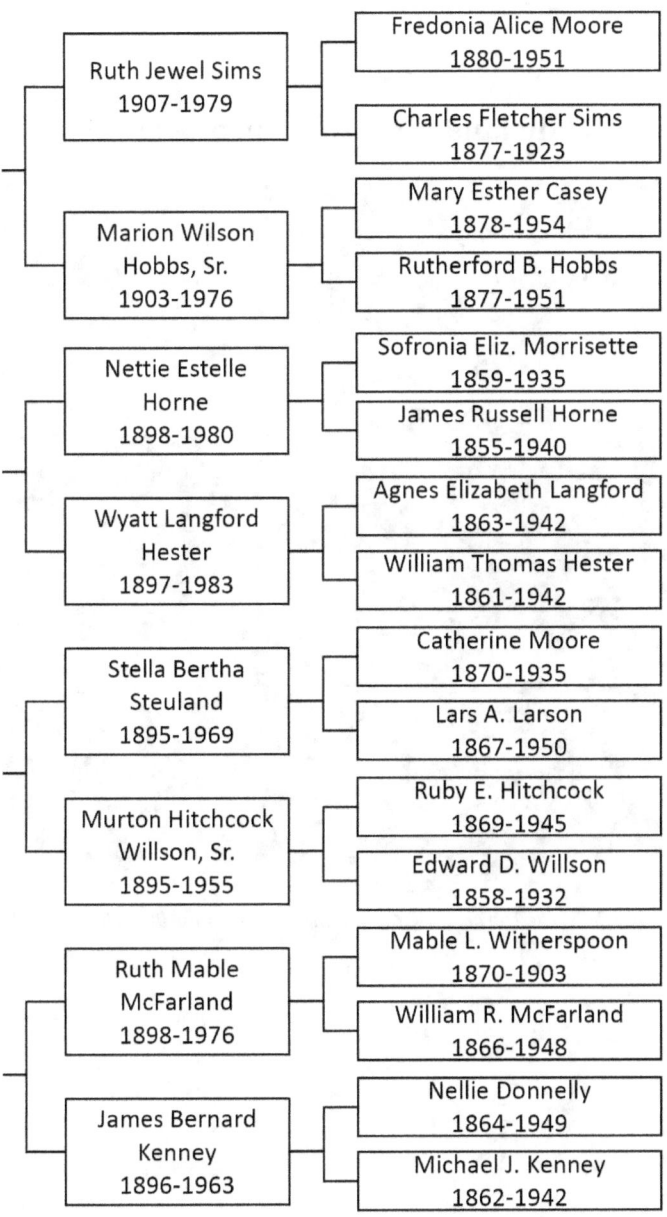

Ruth Jewel Sims
1907-1979

Fredonia Alice Moore
1880-1951

Charles Fletcher Sims
1877-1923

Marion Wilson
Hobbs, Sr.
1903-1976

Mary Esther Casey
1878-1954

Rutherford B. Hobbs
1877-1951

Nettie Estelle
Horne
1898-1980

Sofronia Eliz. Morrisette
1859-1935

James Russell Horne
1855-1940

Wyatt Langford
Hester
1897-1983

Agnes Elizabeth Langford
1863-1942

William Thomas Hester
1861-1942

Stella Bertha
Steuland
1895-1969

Catherine Moore
1870-1935

Lars A. Larson
1867-1950

Murton Hitchcock
Willson, Sr.
1895-1955

Ruby E. Hitchcock
1869-1945

Edward D. Willson
1858-1932

Ruth Mable
McFarland
1898-1976

Mable L. Witherspoon
1870-1903

William R. McFarland
1866-1948

James Bernard
Kenney
1896-1963

Nellie Donnelly
1864-1949

Michael J. Kenney
1862-1942

The James Russell Horne Family

Nettie Estelle Horne, my Grandmother Hester, is the little girl in front

Part Four

Looking Ahead

Stella and her Cousins

Stella Berv

Penny & Teddy
Papadin

Danny Berv

Tara Berv

Pax Berv

Owen Berv

Spencer Berv

Reagan Beard

Reese Beard

Rylan Beard

Eliana Zeiger

Mateo Zeiger

Cooper Sams

Birdie, Langford,
& Cece Hester

Laurel Netting,
honorary cousin

Dearest Stella,

It would be a punishment to try and describe your adorable, hilarious, kind self. I love you for your superb, rock star hair, your smile cracks me up, your curiosity of the world being viewed and experienced from your eyes awes and inspires me. I remember the very first time I held you. A beautiful, fragile little person resting her piercing blue eyes in my arms. I felt like I was being honored with the gift of you being my cousin, in fact, I still am! I love you so much, cutie! And I miss you with all my heart. I'll always be here if you need. XOXO,

Cousin Penny

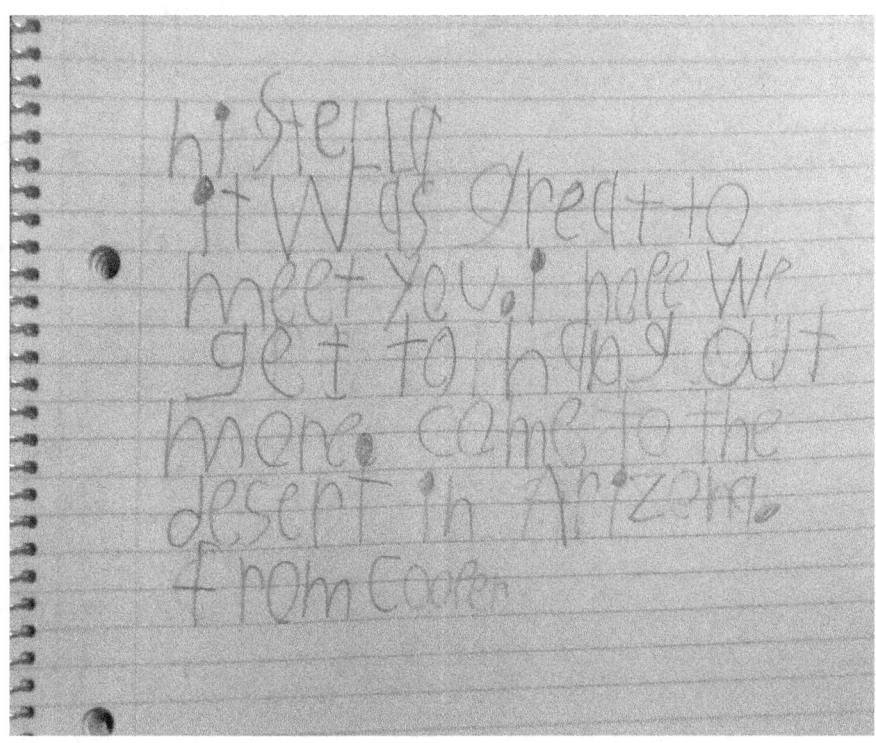

hi Stella
it was great to
meet you. I hope we
get to hang out
more. come to the
desert in Arizona.
from Cooper

Stella,
I love playing Bingo with you
On christmas Eve. I hope
we can do this forever.

Love., Laurel

Part Five

The Binding

A Letter to Stella

WHAT A BEAUTIFUL QUILT covers you, Stella! It's sewn with love, from your people: Nana and Papa, Baba and Pops, Mama and Daddy, aunts and uncles, and the generations preceding them. It's been my pleasure to piece together some squares as well, through friendship, blessing your parents' marriage, and baptizing you as a beloved member of God's family in the community known as Central Presbyterian Church.

One of the powerful images we have for God is "Comforter". While God can't be contained in a single picture, you can rest securely under the strong and grace-stitched blanket that is God's love for you. As you grow and add to its patchwork stories, remember that love from which you can never be separated. Remember that you are never alone, but part of an amazing family who will always welcome you home no matter how far you journey.

May your quilt be a blessing your whole life through, Stella. And may you be a blessing…offering warmth, acceptance, caring— and that winsome smile!—to your family, community, and the wide, wild world.

Stella's baptism

With love,

Pastor Louise Westfall

Acknowledgments

THIS BOOK WOULD NEVER have been written were it not for two people, Ellen Fisher, and Eva Mate. We have met via Zoom, for one hour, two to three mornings a week, for the past eighteen months, and their encouragement and experience moved me along, slowly but surely, from concept to completion. During this period Ellen published her second work of historical fiction and began her third, and Eva—in addition to editing my book and Ellen's—signed a contract for a mystery-romance trilogy. Remarkable women!

Of course, Ellen and I might never have met Eva were it not for former Golf Star Vicki Godbey and her husband HG. Their daughter had attended the University of Colorado with Eva. They learned of Eva's aspiration to establish herself as a writer and editor when HG, a Colorado Golf Hall of Famer, was back in Denver for a visit, and played a round with Eva's husband Ed, Executive Director of the Colorado Golf Association. The Godbeys connected Eva to Ellen, who invited me to join the two of them in the morning meetings Eva labeled "writing sprints". As the writing of this book continually reminded me, we are all connected on some level, a truth that gives added meaning to my life.

Stella's Quilt is, in many ways, about those connections—to friends and family, to our faith communities, and to our professional colleagues. It is about the seemingly random connections we make that turn out not to be random at all.

Andy—my husband, best friend, and head cheerleader—jokes about the way I look for that mutual connection with almost everyone I meet, and about the way I am constantly trying to connect people to each other. That said, he thought it a stretch when I suggested to my friend Barbara that perhaps we should connect her son and our daughter. He worried privately that this might be a quick way to end a lovely friendship between the Bervs and the Kenneys. Today, however, the four of us share a beautiful granddaughter, Stella.

I am grateful to members of the Beard and Berv families for sitting down with me and sharing their memories and their stories. I am honored and humbled by their trust in my ability to handle these with care.

I am grateful to members of my own family, who answered my texts and emails promptly and helped to separate fact from family lore. I thank Bo and Lauren for tenderly correcting my memories, and for understanding that, although my parenting was not perfect, I was always doing the best I could.

I thank Andy for delving into the "Kenney archives" that reside in our basement, and for forgetting—quarter after quarter—to cancel his membership to Ancestry.com, which in the end proved to be so helpful! I thank my good friend Carol Lay, who graduated from TJ with Barbara and Jan, for sharing her high school annual with me.

Even the most casual of readers will note the disparity in length among the "blocks"—in particular, the one about me and my family of birth. This is in no way intended to diminish the Beards and the Bervs, or for that matter, the Kenneys, and their importance to Stella. My stories are simply the ones I know, and I could have written many more. One thing I have learned about Alex and his siblings is that they are all good writers, and I encourage them to take up the mantle and record more of their family's fascinating history.

I am grateful to my many friends, who have continued to ask in such an encouraging way, "How is your book coming along?", that I knew I had to finish it. I have lost dear friends over the course of this project—Sue Wilcox, Rick Shanks, Carol Griesemer, Fritz Hill, John Stamper, Virginia Hawkins, Don Milliman, Gerry Moore, Alan Kirkbride, Bill Newell, and Katie Johnson—each an example of a life well lived, and each a gentle reminder that we do not have unlimited time to accomplish our goals. Three dear family members have passed on—Daddy, Consuelo Hester, and Denise Berv—each an important block of Stella's quilt.

I knew nothing about publishing a book. Fortunately, Veronica Yager, who Ellen recommended, knows everything, and guided me seamlessly through the process—from completed manuscript to book-in-hand. I thank Leanne Harvey, of Mount Vincent Quilts, for giving me permission to print her original *Stella* quilt pattern.

Finally, I am grateful to you, for choosing to read what I have written.

—Sherry Hester Kenney
November 1, 2022